KNIT, KNIT
KNIT

Polly Peebles liked to knit.
She liked to knit things
that someone could wear.
Knit, knit, knit, knit.

Every week,
her friend Sara
came to visit.
"What are you knitting now?"
she asked.

"Socks for my brother,"
said Polly Peebles.
"I like to knit things
that someone can wear."
Knit, knit, knit, knit.

Polly Peebles knitted
so much and so fast
that soon everyone had
all the knitted things they needed.

But Polly Peebles had lots of leftover wool.

Next week,
when Sara came to visit,
Polly Peebles was knitting
something very long.
"Who is that for?" asked Sara.

"I don't know," said Polly Peebles.
"Everyone I know has a scarf.
But what else could I knit
with so many bits
of leftover wool?"
Knit, knit, knit, knit.

Next week,
when Sara came to visit,
Polly Peebles was knitting
some very long socks.
"Who is going to wear them?"
said Sara.

Polly Peebles smiled.

"George is going to wear them,"
she said.
"I got a new pet to wear my scarf.
Now I'm knitting him some socks.

"I like to knit things
that someone can wear."
Knit, knit, knit, knit.

MONOGRAPHS (
SOCIETY FOR RESEA
CHILD DEVELO.

Serial No. 239, Vol. 59, No. 1, 1994

A NEW LOOK AT SOME OLD MECHANISMS IN HUMAN NEWBORNS: TASTE AND TACTILE DETERMINANTS OF STATE, AFFECT, AND ACTION

lass
aro

BY
Barr

ORS

MONOGRAPHS OF THE SOCIETY FOR RESEARCH IN CHILD DEVELOPMENT
Serial No. 239, Vol. 59, No. 1, 1994

CONTENTS

ABSTRACT

Blass, Elliott M., and Ciaramitaro, Vivian. A New Look at Some Old Mechanisms in Human Newborns: Taste and Tactile Determinants of State, Affect, and Action. With Commentary by Ronald G. Barr; and a Reply by Elliott M. Blass and Vivian Ciaramitaro. *Monographs of the Society for Research in Child Development,* 1994, **59**(1, Serial No. 239).

Three studies of normal human newborns and of newborns of methadone-maintained mothers evaluated how orotactile (pacifier) and orogustatory (sucrose) stimulation, alone and in combination, affected crying behavior, heart rate, gross motor activity, eye opening, and hand-mouth coordination. For each measure of infant state, pacifier and sucrose stimulation each caused significant changes that followed very different time courses. Orotactile (pacifier) stimulation precipitated immediate changes in all behaviors, and, when the pacifier was removed, all behaviors soon reverted to baseline levels. The changes precipitated by orogustatory (sucrose) stimulation were more gradual but extended well beyond the end of sucrose administration. Although both pacifier and sucrose influences are mediated orally as opposed to in the stomach or intestine, the effects involve different brain pathways. The fact that infants born to methadone-maintained mothers did not change their behaviors during or after sucrose administration but that their reactions to pacifier stimulation could not be distinguished from those of normal infants suggests that reactions to sucrose are mediated centrally by endogenous opioids while those to the pacifier work through other central mechanisms. These findings with human newborns are consonant with those of many animal studies that have also shown rapid onset and rapid offset for contact- and suckling-induced behavioral changes, slower onset and slower offset for changes induced by taste, and opioid mediation of changes induced by the taste of sucrose. Orogustatory and orotactile influences on affect, action, and cardiovascular function are discussed from the perspectives of energetics and growth, central determinants of state, motivation, and learning during the newborn period.

I. INTRODUCTION: BEHAVIORAL AND BIOLOGICAL CONSEQUENCES OF SUCKLING IN RATS AND HUMANS

A fundamental goal of biological research on ontogeny is to discover when and how developmental changes can be induced as well as the consequences, limits, and mechanisms underlying such changes. With their commitment to defining and understanding environmental influences on behavior, developmental psychology and psychobiology both share these goals. Recent animal studies on avian (Marler, 1991) and mammalian (Leon, 1992) development have identified time frames within which changes in particular behaviors can be induced, the circumstances in which these changes occur, and some of the mechanisms that mediate them. From these studies has emerged an appreciation of both infants' rich capacity for change and the limits placed on change by phylogeny and ecology (Alberts & Cramer, 1988; Blass, 1992, in press; West, King, & Arburg, 1988).

The present *Monograph,* which is concerned with how human mothers influence their infants through nursing, grows out of this research tradition. By approximating the gustatory and tactile stimulation normally provided by the mother through her milk, breast, and nipple, we start to identify and characterize behavioral and cardiac changes that mothers induce in their newborns. Because the characteristics of calming induced by the taste of sucrose in human infants parallel those found in infant rats (findings established by previous research, which we review in subsequent sections), we hypothesized that the effects in both species share a common brain mechanism, specifically, that taste causes a functional change in central opioid mediation.[1] This particular hypothesis was tested in the current studies in

[1] Opioids are families of proteins that are synthesized in every major organ system, including the brain. In the brain and the spinal cord, opioids protect against pain. They also modulate cardiac output and enhance the individual's appetite for fats and sweets. Endorphins constitute one family of opioids. These are primarily detected by a class of receptors called "mμ receptors." There are pharmacological agents—antagonists—that prevent an opioid from binding to its receptor. Naloxone, e.g., is an endorphin antagonist (Martin, 1984).

four infants born to women who were maintained on methadone during pregnancy. These infants, who by virtue of their prenatal history did not have functional opioid systems, were not calmed by sucrose. This led us to conclude that human mothers, like rat mothers, calm their infants during nursing by both orogustatory and orotactile stimulation and that the two kinds of stimulation are mediated by separate mechanisms. Taste influences infant behavior and state through central systems that have an opioid component; tactile stimulation uses other neurochemical pathways that have not yet been identified. The implications of these findings for infant motivation and for the development of the mother-infant relationship are discussed from the infant's perspective in the concluding chapter.

THE PROTOTYPICAL SETTING

The newborn cries on awakening. Her mother approaches her, fondles her, picks her up, perhaps engages her in play or some other form of stimulation, and finally nurses her. Crying stops and does not resume even after nursing has ended. The infant lies awake and alert and may attend to parents, siblings, or objects surrounding her. Eventually, she goes to sleep, and the cycle begins again.

This cycle and its participants are familiar. The scenario described above captures the essential features of human infant-mother interactions—indeed, it describes important segments of mother-infant interactions of all mammals (Gubernick & Klopfer, 1981). Furthermore, on a closer examination of its components and of the consequences of the interactions between the players, the full richness of the infant's behavior becomes apparent. This richness invites the identification and exploration of infants' behavioral and physiological cycles, of short-term alterations of state and behavior within the larger cycles, of the mother's contributions to these changes, and of the lasting effects of and mechanisms underlying these changes. With some luck, the principles of organization that govern growth, energy conservation, and behavioral change might emerge from these examinations. In this spirit, the studies and reflections shared in this *Monograph* first identify stimuli by means of which human mothers can influence their newborn's state and then characterize the mechanisms underlying these changes. The studies that we report here are based on animal experiments that have identified endogenous opioids as potential contributors to state changes through selective opioid blockade (Kehoe & Blass, 1986a, 1986b, 1986c) and extend those findings to include human infants born to women who were maintained on methadone during pregnancy.

The analyses that we have undertaken are based on three simple (perhaps obvious) assumptions. First, mammalian mothers calm their agitated newborns in one (or both) of two ways: either generally through whole-body contact (i.e., warmth, texture, gentle pressure, rocking) or specifically through nursing. Nursing calms the infant by means of the milk delivered to her, the touch of the nipple or breast inside her mouth, and the motor patterns elicited in her by the delivery of milk or by nipple or breast stimulation. The calm state is biologically significant for the infant because it maximizes energy conservation. Second, changes in state caused by these events contribute to long-term behavioral change. In particular, they allow human and animal infants to learn about both the individual and the circumstances that cause state changes. Finally, stimuli that predict state changes acquire enduring affective significance, with the result that infants find them attractive, orient toward them, and may become distressed if they are removed or if they lose their predictive significance.

Within this framework, the current studies evaluated the effectiveness of orogustatory and orotactile stimulation as agents of state change in human newborns. The natural situation of mothers holding their infants to nurse them, and thereby providing rich physical contact and a particular context, was simplified by focusing on two fundamental aspects of nursing—the tactile sensation of a nipple stimulating the mouth, tongue, and palate and the taste of sucrose in both the presence and the absence of nipple stimulation (our choice of a sucrose solution will be justified below). Our choice of paradigm was not intended to preclude or diminish the importance of other factors inherent in the nursing situation—it simply focuses on oral contributions to calming and state change in newborns.

BACKGROUND

The present studies emerged from demonstrations that, in infant rats, the tastes of sucrose and milk markedly reduce crying and raise the pain threshold (Blass & Fitzgerald, 1988; Blass, Fitzgerald, & Kehoe, 1987). This occurs even in newborn rats, which have never suckled (Blass, Jackson, & Smotherman, 1991). These changes caused by oral stimuli support classical conditioning in that olfactory and tactile stimuli associated with these changes gain control over particular behavioral patterns. That is, in the presence of a conditioned odor or taste stimulus, rats behave as if they are receiving infusions of sugar or milk (Johanson, Hall, & Polefrone, 1984; Johanson & Teicher, 1980; Shide & Blass, 1991; for reviews, see Hall, 1990; and Johanson & Terry, 1988).

To the extent that humans and rats share parallel behavioral, physiological, and anatomical processes in the service of lactation, growth, ingestive control, and possibly simple conditioning, we sought to determine whether these parallels also extended to the immediate calming and pain-reducing consequences of ingestion and to their underlying mechanisms. A more informed and complete appreciation of the behavioral complexity of newborn humans will provide a richer understanding of processes underlying physical growth and differentiation, of how early behavioral state changes may occur, and of the particular consequences of these changes. An understanding of the newborn's range of behavioral adjustments, within the context of physiological alterations induced by the mother, may help us trace developmentally events that might give rise to long-term behavioral change.

Efforts to understand the means of calming infants are not new to either psychology or pediatrics. Practitioners have long been aware of the need to calm and stabilize infants for both pediatric and medical evaluation. Calming their infants is, of course, among the premier concerns of parents, especially during the early months. Because holding, rocking, and comforting infants is such an intuitive facet of caregiving, physical contact is widely recognized as contributing to the baby's comfort. This emphasis on physical contact has received scientific validation in the form of the justly famous studies of Harlow and his colleagues of the importance of contact and stability for growth and emotional development (Harlow & Harlow, 1965).

Unfortunately, exploring this one aspect of a mother's influence on her infant has led to the underrepresentation of others, especially in newborn humans. In particular, the behavioral consequences of receiving milk have remained largely unexplored. This is regrettable since it is well known that human infant gustation very strongly resembles that of human adults as judged behaviorally through changes in ingestive pattern and intake, especially of the sugars (for reviews, see Cowart, 1981; Crook, 1978; Desor, Maller, & Turner, 1973; Maller & Desor, 1973). Yet, to our knowledge, studies of flavors have not been undertaken in newborn infants. Doing so would be particularly interesting in the case of fats because, when somewhat stressed, both adult humans and adult rats preferentially ingest sweets and fats (Marks-Kaufman, Plager, & Kanarek, 1985).

It is worth briefly reviewing the animal and human infant experiments on behavioral reactions to gustatory stimulation, for both are germane to the current research. Our earliest investigations of taste and behavior in neonatal rats, which focused on calming (as defined by changes in ultrasonic vocalization) and pain endurance (as defined by changes in pain threshold) caused by milk ingestion, were guided by three independent lines of animal and human research on behavioral and pharmacological adjustments to stress and pain. One body of literature dealt with opioid modulation of pain. Morphine, of course, is a very potent pain-reducing agent that acts both in the brain and in the spinal cord and whose effectiveness is linearly related to dose (Olson, Olson, & Kastin, 1987, 1989). Its pharmacological effectiveness is blocked by pretreatment with naloxone (i.e., the mμ receptor antagonist). Systemic or brain injections of naloxone or of its longer-acting derivative, naltrexone, allow one to assess the mechanisms underlying calming or analgesia induced by naturally occurring exchanges between mother and infant. Thus, if a mechanism that underlies behavioral change operates, in part, through endorphins, then injecting an animal with naloxone will prevent that mechanism from functioning, and the behavioral effect will be attenuated or blocked. When we began our studies in 1984, enough was known about the pharmacology and the central anatomy of pain and stress systems in both animals and humans to provide a foundation for pharmacological and behavioral explorations in infants.

Within the context of behaviorally functional opioid development,[2] an important study by Stickrod, Kimble, and Smotherman (1982) demonstrated behavioral sensitivity to another class of opioids, the enkephalins. Stickrod et al. gained surgical access to 20-day-old rat fetuses (pregnancy is normally about 21 days in albino rats) and injected apple juice into the amniotic fluid, which was swallowed by the fetuses. After a suitable interval, they then injected *5-met*-enkephalin into the fetuses's peritoneal cavity. The females delivered these pups normally and raised them without further experimental manipulation. At 15 days of age, the investigators allowed the rats to drink apple juice and measured fluid intake; animals that had received the pairing of apple juice and *5-met*-enkephalin as fetuses drank significantly more apple juice than control rats did.

This finding held a number of important implications for future research. First, it confirmed that, in rats, late-term fetuses can taste (and/or smell). Second, it demonstrated that this sensory information was available for the prediction of or association with certain events, in particular with changes in opioid status, which presumably engaged brain reward systems. Third, the memory of the fetal event persisted for a long time ex utero and survived the natural experiences of the nest, which provide rich memories of their own. The Stickrod et al. (1982) study was also significant because it directed attention toward the possibility that the mother might affect infant state from birth by modulating the infant's own opioid systems through contact or milk delivery (or both).

The second line of study relevant to our current work explored the fact that, in humans and rats, mild stress enhances appetite (Marks-Kaufman &

[2] "Behaviorally functional development" means that the anatomical, physiological, and neurochemical components of a mechanism have matured to a level at which the system can mediate the processes (e.g., conditioning) or behaviors that they underlie. In principle, prior to that point, the system will not function normally because its underlying brain elements have not reached critical junctures in their own development. The underlying elements do not have to be at adult levels of maturity in order for the system to be functional. Thus, in utero conditioning occurred despite the fact that central opioid systems are operating at a level only 30% of that of mature adults.

Kanarek, 1981). The enhancement is interesting because it is selective for fats and sweets; other foods are not preferentially eaten (Marks-Kaufman et al., 1985). Moreover, naloxone blocked enhanced feeding at low doses that did not interfere with spontaneous ingestion or with deprivation-induced feeding. This, too, is relevant because it points to endogenous opioids as possible mediators of the calming properties of sugar and fat in adults and invites exploration of its causes and developmental time course.

A third influential body of work concerned the effects of stress on pain responsivity in adults. This is a complex literature that is only now starting to be integrated along behavioral and pharmacological lines (Maier, 1989). For present purposes, it is enough to say that stress-induced pain reduction (antinociception) is a strong and reliable phenomenon that is highly replicable among laboratories and that, under certain conditions, is opioid mediated. Determining the circumstances under which stress and pain systems interact and the mechanisms underlying such interactions is important. Behavioral changes in response to stress are central to an animal's ability to cope with later, independent painful events. Thus, for example, Maier found that rats that had experienced foot shock were more tolerant of painful heat stimulation of the tail than control rats were. The number of shocks and the time separating shock presentation from heat stimulation determined the level of stress-induced analgesia and whether it was opioid or nonopioid mediated. Evidence of such enduring adjustments to stress caused by opioid release encouraged us to seek changes in infant state and behavior induced by natural positive stimulation such as milk, sucrose, or fat that could cause the release of endogenous opioids.

ANIMAL STUDIES

The confluence of these three lines of study led to the following questions, which guided our earlier work with animals: Can infants respond to changes in circulating opioids? If they can, do any natural events have consequences for newborns that are mediated by changes in endogenous opioid systems? Can these changes be linked to external, neutral stimuli in a way that will cause a reorganization of behavior—that is, have enduring developmental effects? We now briefly review the findings of this research.

The initial studies by Kehoe and Blass (1986a, 1986b, 1986c, 1986d) demonstrated that, in isolated, 10-day-old infant rats, morphine injections decreased ultrasonic vocalizations and increased the latency with which a forelimb was retracted from a 48°C surface. As expected, the effects were blocked by injections of the morphine antagonist naloxone. Interestingly, isolation alone mimicked the pain-reducing effects of morphine injections: relative to nonisolated siblings, paw-retraction latencies were elevated in isolates, and this difference between siblings was also eliminated by naloxone injections. Moreover, the number of vocalizations emitted by isolates was markedly increased by this opioid antagonist, suggesting that calling levels were normally suppressed, possibly to prevent advertisement of an individual's or litter's position.

Additional studies showed that morphine injections were rewarding: they increased later intake of fluids associated with the injection and caused animals to prefer the side of a maze bearing an odor that had predicted the injections' occurrence. These effects were prevented from developing by injecting naloxone prior to conditioning and hence preventing morphine from activating its receptors (Kehoe & Blass, 1986b). The expression of a preference was also prevented by naloxone injection at the time of testing (Kehoe & Blass, 1989). The implications of this finding will be discussed later.

There was reason to believe that a common mechanism was shared by both the stress and the pain systems because changes in vocalization and pain threshold were highly correlated (r = .69–.83, depending on experimental condition; Kehoe & Blass, 1986d). The systems mediating changes in calm and pain appeared to be located in the brain, not the periphery, because injecting naloxone into the ventricles of the brain, in doses that were ineffective when injected into the body, fully reversed the analgesic and calming effects of morphine (Kehoe & Blass, 1986c). Reciprocally, injecting morphine into the ventricles was calming and relieved pain. These studies in infant rats called attention to central motive systems that, among other things, were opioid mediated, stress sensitive, calming, and antinociceptive (pain reducing).

Was there a biological basis for these phenomena, or were they pharmacological in nature (i.e., due either to concentrations or rates of delivery that exceed physiological levels)? A series of subsequent studies demonstrated that sucrose infused into the rat's mouth reduced vocalizations and enhanced paw-lift latencies (Blass et al., 1987), as did milk (Blass & Fitzgerald, 1988), fat, and the carbohydrate Polycose (Shide & Blass, 1989). In all instances, the calming and pain-reducing effects of the oral infusions were attenuated or fully blocked by injecting naloxone prior to infusion. These studies also held implications for infant learning and motivation. Infant rats that had an otherwise aversive odor paired with oral infusions of sucrose or fat exhibited a preference for that odor (Shide & Blass, 1991); however, when sucrose or fat was infused into the mouth following naloxone pretreatment, the preference for the associated odor disappeared. Moreover, when naloxone preceded testing, it prevented expression of the conditioned preference. Thus, smelling the conditioned odor either caused the release of endogenous opioids or sensitized the central detection system in rats for whom the odor had predicted taste- (or flavor-) induced central changes.

Accordingly, these studies converged to show that a number of foods and fluids could readily influence infant rat behavior and that these state changes were easily brought under the control of different odors or tastes by conditioning. Some of these substances were of a composition similar to (or were components of) mother's milk. Hence, it seems reasonable to suggest that naturally occurring gustatory and postabsorptive changes triggered by the mother through her milk could offer a constellation of stimuli that provide a biological foundation for positive affect toward the dam. The opioid-stress-pain system did not depend on standard postnatal experiences for its expression. Indeed, it was present at birth, as shown by Blass et al. (1991), who demonstrated marked pain reduction by a single 20-μl injection of milk into the mouths of rat pups that had been cesarean delivered within minutes of testing and had never had contact with an adult female, let alone suckled.

HUMAN INFANT STUDIES

These findings and considerations naturally led us to initiate parallel investigations of human infant affective responses to sweet and other tastes. The literature was helpful here because the hedonics of gustation in human infants had received attention at least from the time of Darwin (1877). Newborns and possibly even fetuses (DeSnoo, 1937) respond positively to sweet. In fact, no obvious differences between infant and adult responses to sugars have been reported. Sucrose preference, for example, as measured by intake, is linearly related to concentration at all ages; rank ordering of sugar palatability by adults and by infants was shown to be identical across a number of sugars with sucrose preferred to fructose, which was preferred to glucose, which was preferred to lactose (Desor et al., 1973). It had not been established, however, whether the mechanisms that gave rise to positive affect in laboratory tests were also engaged during the normal course of exchanges between mother and infant and, if they were, whether they could protect the child against pain and stress. The earlier gustatory studies, which did not have the frame of reference provided by the recent animal studies, could not pose the question. Nevertheless, these studies have contributed significantly to our understanding of the development of affect (Lipsitt, 1977; Lipsitt, Reilly, Butcher, & Greenwood, 1976), and it is unfortunate that these contributions have not been granted their empirical or theoretical due, having been seen as speaking only to sensory development.

Even so, however, taste studies in human infants have provided information that is central to any developmental synthesis of suckling, mother-infant interactions, and affect. First, at birth (and probably before), infants have a well-developed coding process that discriminates among different pure substances and that, within a substance, distinguishes among concentrations (Crook, 1978; Desor et al., 1973). Second, this sensory system has access to a variety of motor systems—reflexive, instrumental, and communicative—that can be influenced either to accept or to reject a substance (Chiva, 1982; Steiner, 1979), can lead to more rapid ingestion (Lipsitt & Kaye, 1965), can be used as an operant for obtaining fluids, and may communicate acceptance or rejection of a tastant (Steiner, 1979).

Although the implications of these findings for early learning and affect were debated, their import was discarded since the view that infants were very incompletely formed adults held sway at the time (Campbell & Coultier, 1976; Sameroff, 1972). Such dismissal is understandable within the context of then-prevalent opinions that newborns had only the most rudimentary forms of sensorimotor integration and that their cognitive capacities to extract relations from, or provide structure to, the environment were more limited (Piaget, 1952). It was also consistent with the prevailing medical view that infants' emotional-motivational systems were poorly developed and that infant responses were entirely peripheral and reflexive in nature—hence, it was assumed that infants could not experience either pleasure or distress (Pieper, 1963).

Informed by more recent thinking as well as by our own work, our reading of this early literature is that the sensory and motor phases of the gustatory system in the human infant are well developed (Mistretta & Bradley, 1988) and that that system is available to interact with perceptual and motivational systems to guide and sustain behavior (Hogan, 1988). In principle, these motivational systems make organized behavioral systems accessible to the relevant learning and memory capacities available to infants at birth (Johanson et al., 1984). In other words, we speculated that the gustatory system might lead infants to learn about the particularities of the individual who delivers food or other aspects of health care. This learning is founded on gustatory properties of food that engage broader motivational systems and permits the perception of available visual, auditory, tactile, and olfactory stimulation provided by the caretaker (Blass, Ganchrow, & Steiner, 1984; E. M. Blass & L. B. Hoffmeyer, unpublished findings [cited in Blass, 1990]; Bushnell, Sai, & Mullin, 1983; Rosenblatt, 1983).

The motivation, learning, and memory capacities that are engaged during normal infant-mother interactions are central to lasting changes. Beginning in 1976, the view of infant incompetence changed radically as animal research repeatedly demonstrated that infant rats utilized their conditioning and cognitive abilities to extract order from settings made seemingly unpredictable by the fact that nest, food, and milk odors vary from mother to mother and depend seasonally on available foods (Amsel, Burdette, & Letz, 1976; Johanson & Hall, 1979; Kenny & Blass, 1977). Cross-setting diversity is overcome when animals that are dependent on odor cues for suckling

(Hofer, Shair, & Singh, 1976; Teicher & Blass, 1976) link prenatal with postnatal odors prior to their initial suckling bout (Pedersen & Blass, 1982).

Although it is central to this *Monograph,* suckling was not the only behavior that was found either to depend on or to have access to learning and memory processes during early development. The network of early behaviors subject to modification by nest experience proved so widespread that, in 1983, Rosenblatt could write that at least infant rats and kittens were able to negotiate their immediate worlds on the basis of tactile and olfactory information derived from close contact with mother and siblings—they were not naive about their environment every time they ventured into it (Rosenblatt, 1983). In fact, infants of these species appear to use specialized rules to find out about the world in which they function (Alberts & Cramer, 1988; Blass, 1992).

The earlier underestimation of human infants' cognitive capacities is also now widely appreciated (Spelke, Breinlinger, Macomber, & Jacobson, 1992), and even a brief summary of what is now recognized to be their cognitive and perceptual abilities would take us too far afield. Suffice it to say that, for our part, we no longer wanted to underestimate the capacities of newborn humans or to miss detecting possible opportunities that infants may use to bring information to their extant and developing cognitive systems, such as facial discrimination and perception (Bushnell et al., 1983; Johnson, Dziurawiec, Ellis, & Morton, 1991; Morton & Johnson, 1991).

With this in mind, we focused on the following questions: What are the natural events that cause infant state change (for our particular inquiries, calming)? What are the central mechanisms underlying these changes? Can the infant identify certain features of the caretaker that consistently predict positive change, and, if so, on what basis are these features identified? Finally, would studies of the very early reactions of infants to the taste of sucrose and to the presence of a pacifier start to reveal the organization of motivation underlying the mother-infant relationship?

Combined with our previous findings in other species, these questions allowed us to develop a rational approach to the study of affect in human newborns. We began by providing newborns (1–2 days of age), who were spontaneously crying and obviously distressed, with microliter volumes of a 12% sucrose solution via syringe at a rate of 0.1 ml/min, and we established scoring systems on the basis of the infants' behavior. Six major findings emerged from these initial studies (Blass, Fillion, Rochat, Hoffmeyer, & Metzger, 1989; Rochat, Blass, & Hoffmeyer, 1988; Smith, Fillion, & Blass, 1990). First, crying stopped within 2 min of the administration of sucrose, that is, after a total of 0.2 ml (200 μl). Second, crying did not recur until well beyond the time of sucrose administration. In fact, it recurred only very occasionally, and quiescence was the rule during the 5-min period that followed sucrose termination. Third, infants did not go to sleep; on the contrary, their eyes often opened wide, and they remained calm and alert. Fourth, this calming effect could not be attributed to sucking the syringe or to the receipt of fluid per se because water administered by the same means was ineffective. Fifth, a completely unexpected behavior emerged: infants who received sucrose placed their hands in their mouths. Hand-in-mouth behavior appeared only *after* crying had stopped and the infant had calmed; it invariably disappeared once sucrose administration was terminated, yet the calm persisted.

Sixth, sucrose administration differentially affected spontaneous patterns of newborns' ingestive behavior. Figure 1 depicts mean mouthing behavior (dotted line) and mean hand-mouth contact before, during, and after the period of sucrose administration ($N = 13$ newborns). Sucrose enhanced both mouthing and hand-mouth behavior, although in different ways. Mouthing started to increase within 5 sec of presentation of sucrose—probably the time necessary for neural transmission and motor recruitment—and it tapered off gradually during the 110-sec interval between sucrose deliveries to attain its new, elevated baseline levels. Hand-mouth coordination was elevated throughout the sucrose phase of the experiment. Unlike mouthing, however, its occurrence did not track individual instances of sucrose presentation. Hand-mouth behavior appears to reflect both state (the infants were agitated) and situational (they were receiving sucrose intermittently) factors, whereas mouthing was determined in addition by the immediate local event of sucrose delivery. Different patterns and time courses of change imply that different underlying central mechanisms were engaged by sucrose taste. By following the strategy of closely scrutinizing multiple changes induced by taste and texture, the current experiments determine how the taste of sucrose and the presence of a pacifier each orchestrate a number of different behavioral and physiological systems in newborns. Under natural mother-infant exchanges, these systems may act in concert to conserve energy. Attention to the differential effects of taste or tactile stimulation may identify the specific components of motivational systems, their organization, and their underlying mechanisms.

THE CURRENT EXPERIMENTS

Our previous studies of rats and humans did not provide us with sufficient information on the different ways in which gustation could affect newborns' behavior. They did implicate the opioid systems in mediating taste-induced change, however. This provided the basis for the current studies because the opioid systems are ancient phylogenetically and are integral to the functioning of every major physiological system that has been studied. Of particular additional interest to us were the effects of opioids

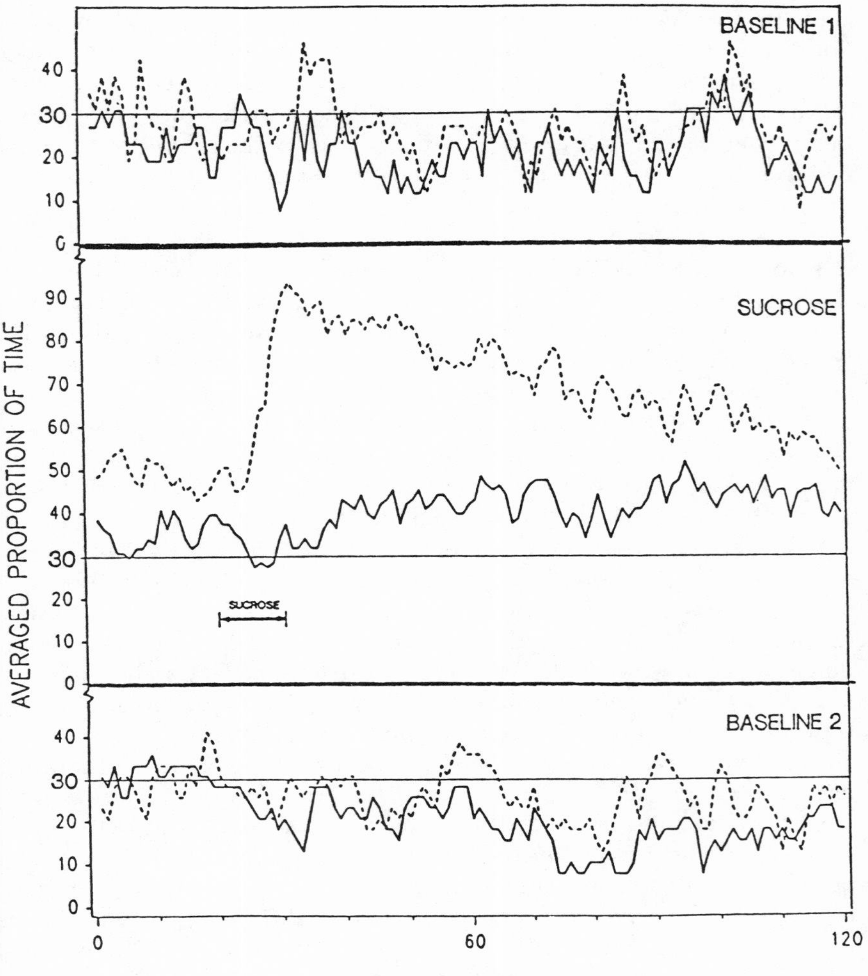

Fig. 1.—Average proportion of time spent in mouthing (dashed lines) and hand-mouth behaviors (solid lines) in 13 newborn infants. Because each cycle of sucrose delivery (10-sec time bar) lasted 2 min, the 6-min prestimulation baseline (baseline 1) and the 14-min poststimulation baseline (baseline 2) periods are also presented as 2-min blocks of time. Thus, by dividing the 14-min poststimulation period into seven 2-min blocks and averaging the incidence of occurrence for each 5-sec epoch across infants, we see, e.g., that a mean of 34% of the time was spent mouthing during the 55–60-sec epoch. The solid bar at 30 sec represents the mean time spent mouthing during the prestimulation period. Mouthing behavior increased well above its baseline level (note the proportion of mouthing prior to sucrose delivery) during the 10 min of sucrose stimulation, and it increased dramatically during each 2-min cycle with sucrose administration. Hand-mouth behavior also increased above its own baseline during the sucrose phase of the experiment, but, unlike mouthing behavior, there was no obvious cyclicity in its occurrence. (Figure 1 is taken from Blass et al., 1989.)

on cardiovascular output and on gross motor activity: if sweet taste functions to reduce energy expenditure, then sucrose should decrease heart rate and activity. (It should also be borne in mind that opioids influence gastric motility by relaxing the gastrointestinal tract [Porocca, Mosberg, Hurst, Hruby, & Burks, 1984] and promoting nutrient absorption; evaluating this function, however, is beyond our capacity.) Furthermore, because the nursing setting provides an opportunity for newborns to learn about the particular features of their mother, it follows that their eyes should open while sucking a pacifier or tasting a sweet solution. Accordingly, eye opening was also evaluated in the current studies.

Our earlier analyses were incomplete in two other significant ways. First, only distressed infants were studied—the effects of sucrose on the behavior of infants in the predominant quiescent state simply had not been evaluated in our paradigm. Second, with a single exception, our previous studies focused on the effects of taste on stress and pain. In the present experiments, we more systematically evaluated the effects of orotactile stimulation as provided by a pacifier on various aspects of infant behavior and physiology when the pacifier is presented alone and together with sucrose. This provides a first approximation of the biologically natural setting in which tactile stimulation gives rise to, and combines with, gustatory stimulation. Finally, because of our interest in the mechanisms underlying the mother-infant interactions that mediate calming, we studied in depth the reactions shown to sucrose and to a pacifier by four infants born to women who were maintained on methadone during their pregnancy.

II. METHODS OF THE CURRENT STUDIES

SUBJECTS

The 28 female and 36 male subjects in this study were born in Jamaica Hospital in Queens, New York. The hospital serves a lower-middle-class to poverty-level catchment area. Infants were the products of normal, uneventful pregnancies and were delivered either vaginally or by elective cesarean section. All mothers had either attended a prenatal clinic or been seen by local obstetricians during pregnancy. According to mothers' self-reports, no drugs of abuse were utilized during pregnancy; urine screens of both mother and infant were negative for cocaine. Twenty-one of the infants were African-American, 22 of Hispanic origin, 6 Caucasian, and 15 Oriental. The major differences in virtually all demographic aspects between this population and the middle- to upper-middle-class urban and suburban infants that we had studied in Baltimore (as well as the rural Caucasian cohort that we are developing in Ithaca, NY) allow for potentially interesting comparisons among populations and, as will be shown, among institutions (in terms of capacity to deliver nursing care).

DESIGN

The study consisted of eight groups of infants derived from a 2 (crying status: agitated vs. calm) × 2 (pacifier vs. syringe delivery) × 2 (sucrose vs. water) design. Infants were designated as either agitated (Experiment 1) or calm (Experiment 2) according to the following criteria. Each infant was evaluated for a maximum of 10 min before entry into the experimental phase. Infants who cried for 36 sec or more for each of 2 consecutive min were placed in the agitated group. This cutoff (i.e., 60%) was selected to provide a stable baseline of crying behavior and, presumably, of the concomitant measures for the agitated group. If this level of crying did not appear during the 10-min period, and if the baby was awake, he or she was assigned to the calm group. As it turned out, infants in the calm group simply did not cry during the 2 min preceding testing. Assignment to pacifier or syringe and to water or sucrose conditions was random. Infants were studied only after parents' informed consent was obtained in the presence of a witness; the consent rate was 63%.

PROCEDURE

All testing took place in a separate room in the hospital nursery. A nurse or physician was always immediately available in the event of any problems arising during the experiment; in fact, this necessary precaution did not have to be utilized during any of the tests that were performed. The infants were brought in their bassinets from the nursery to the test room. They were unswaddled, their diapers changed, and contact electrodes for recording heart rate (Contour Medical Technology, Inc., cardiac monitor leads) gently attached to the chest and connected to a IV4 Biomedical Systems heart rate monitor. Heart rate was recorded every 10 sec by the experimenter, who read the values off a monitor.

The infants remained in their bassinets, loosely covered by a blanket that allowed the free movement of their arms and legs. The 10–18-min experimental period began. Infants were observed until the crying or quiet criteria were reached. They then received either sucrose or water from a syringe or from a coated pacifier. The sucrose solution was made up daily by adding sterile water to 12 grams of sucrose until 100 cc of solution were obtained. Sterile water was given to infants in the water groups. For syringe delivery, either the sucrose solution or water was administered once per minute, at body temperature, in a volume of 0.1 cc over the course of 10 sec. Each infant received five such treatments, once during each of 5 consecutive min; a 3-min period then followed during which no solutions were administered. At the end of testing, the cardiac electrodes were disconnected and the babies reswaddled and returned in their bassinets to the nursery.

After completing the baseline period, infants in the pacifier condition received a pacifier that had been dipped in either the 12% sucrose solution or water. A freshly dipped pacifier was inserted into the infant's mouth once per minute for 5 min in an effort to maintain experimental protocols that paralleled those of groups that received solution by syringe. We recognize that the parallel is not exact since the active sucking of a pacifier precludes crying, a condition that could not arise for the syringe groups. However, infants can and do spit out pacifiers when they are upset or in pain. Moreover, even granting that comparisons made within the crying measure during stimulation may be compromised, comparisons made within the other measures that we used are not constrained by the act of sucking.

Each entire session was recorded on a Panasonic video camera (Model AG-180) connected to a television monitor. The picture was monitored during recording and camera angles and distances adjusted to ensure that the entire infant appeared on the monitor. A stopwatch built into the camera was synchronized with one that the experimenter had in her hand and was used to dictate the timing of the experiment. The camera stopwatch appeared in the video record and facilitated subsequent scoring. In 39% of the sessions, the experimenter was blind as to whether water or sucrose was delivered. Examination of the records showed no differences in outcome and no obvious procedural differences between sessions when the experimenter was informed of and those when she was blind to substance delivery.

SCORING

Five measures were derived from the records: crying, gross activity, hand-in-mouth behavior, heart rate, and eye opening. Notes taken during the experimental procedure were referred to only after all the data from all the infants had been analyzed. Each tape was scored by at least two individuals, both blind as to treatment, with each individual being responsible for evaluating different measures. In our judgment, this procedure reduces scoring bias because it minimizes familiarity with the infant's overall behavioral pattern and maintains the scorer's interest in each infant. Thus, one individual scored crying and hand-mouth behavior while a second scored activity. Heart rate was recorded during a third viewing of the tape, sometimes by the scorers of that infant and sometimes by others, and eye opening was scored last by a different scorer. All measures were scored in 10-sec intervals.

Intra- and interrater reliability was checked on every eighth infant (N = 8). All Pearson r correlations were high, ranging from .82 for activity to .96 for heart rate. The criteria that we used to classify each of the five behaviors under study are given below.

Crying

The scoring notation that we had used in our earlier studies was also used here. Crying was scored as present if a crying sound was heard and a crying face was concurrently observed. Since for present purposes we did not distinguish among different forms of crying, both a whimper and a full-throated cry were scored as crying. Our decision not to draw distinctions among different forms of crying was based on two reasons. First, as we have shown in previous work (and will confirm below), the calming effect of sucrose is profound and essentially stops all crying. Second, it is not clear that there are functional (qualitative) differences among different kinds of crying in newborns, either as to the cause of the crying or as to the caregiver's responsivity. The distinctions might prove worthwhile in future studies in which calming agents that are not as potent as either sucrose or a pacifier are used and when the effects are consequently more subtle.

Hand-Mouth

In an earlier study (Blass et al., 1989), we distinguished between hand-in-mouth and hand-at-mouth behaviors. We have abandoned that distinction here for two main reasons. First, the differentiation is often difficult to make—for example, if an infant has turned her head and her face is hiding the hand contacting the mouth. Second, the functional significance of the distinction is obscure; the only systematic difference that we had established between the two measures was that heavier infants often did not get their hands all the way into their mouths, generally stopping at the perioral region. Accordingly, for ease and reliability of scoring, hand-mouth was scored if the hand was actually in the mouth or if it was at the perioral zone, defined by the sensory field of the trigeminal nerve as demarcated by an imaginary moustache that extended downward to the jaw. For hand-mouth to be scored, the hand had to remain in contact with this zone for at least 1 sec.

Similarly, we have not distinguished in the present study between origins of contact—that is, between the hand coming to the mouth and the mouth moving to the hand—because the functional significance of the different origins is not clear at this point, although it may become so in older infants or in those suffering from different forms of brain damage or drug histories. For the sake of completeness, however, let us note that we have routinely observed three classes of hand-mouth contact in our various studies. The most common among them is hand initiated. In these instances, the head is generally immobile and the hands active; the elbows are typically tucked in close to the infant's sides, and movement originates in the elbow and the wrist. The hand will contact the mouth, and, depending on the infant's state at the start of the experiment, the mouth may or may not open. Occasionally, the mouth opens in advance of hand contact. This may be a case of anticipation as Butterworth (1986) claims, or it may simply reflect the expression of a complex, centrally driven motor sequence analogous to ones described by Fentress (1978) in mice in which head actions are not dependent on tactile stimulation by the forepaw. A second pattern is that in which the hands remain relatively quiescent and the infant reaches toward her hands with her mouth open. This pattern is far less common, although very engaging to observe. In the third pattern, both hand and head move, and a synchrony is established between the two as the infant moves from an agitated to a calm state. As we noted earlier (and discuss below), hand-mouth behavior in newborns is dramatic and its development worthy of detailed study as it may provide insights into the origin of action (Hofsten, 1984, 1989).

Activity

We scored activity using a five-point scale (0–4) adapted from a similar scale devised by Hall (1979) to capture activity changes during feeding in infant rats. The scale points were defined as follows:

0 = no movement occurred except for occasional twitches or limb jerks.

1 = sustained movement (for 2–3 sec or more) of one hand occurred. For example, 1 was scored if the origin of movement was from the elbow or from the shoulder; movements originating from the wrist or the fingers in the absence of elbow or shoulder activity were not counted. Also, the scoring system was "yes-no" and not graded; thus, an infant who moved her hand for only 2–3 sec during a 10-sec scoring period received the same "score" as an infant who made the corresponding movement for the full period.

2 = both arms were active during any part of the 10-sec period, or there was a combination of activity from one arm and either the head (or the body) or the legs. In our experience, either there was no leg movement, or both legs moved.

3 = both the arms and either the head (or body) or the legs were active.

4 = the entire baby was in motion. This is a very rare event, one that occurs in normal newborn humans only under circumstances of extreme crying and agitation. It was common, however, in the infants born to methadone-maintained women.

The advantages of this system for assessing level of activity are its simplicity, reliability, and sensitivity. It did, in fact, capture changes in gross motor activity caused by sucrose or water administered by pacifier or syringe. Furthermore, it was used reliably by a number of undergraduate students at Cornell, who learned the system quickly and accurately. However, there are also disadvantages to this system. First, quantitative information was lost because we did not grade an activity within each 10-sec frame but merely recorded whether it occurred (for 2–3 sec) or not. We are not very concerned about this problem because level of activity as a reflection of state was enduring. Patterns of high (3 or 4) or low (0) activity occurred in relatively long bursts that were often stable for 10–20 sec. Intermediate levels of activity (1 or 2) tended to be episodic, occurring in 3–6 sec bursts. For the purposes of this experiment, quantitative calibration within a 10-sec epoch would have made scoring (limbs × time) unwieldy. Second, and of greater concern, is that the system does not permit pattern recognition. When the videotape records were played back quickly, definite patterns of hand, elbow, or shoulder coordination became apparent, as did patterns of integration between hand and mouth. With the availability of computer-assisted scoring capacities, analysis of such patterns in newborns and older infants holds considerable promise for determining the origins of action and their developmental histories (Thelen & Ulrich, 1991).

Eye Opening

Eye opening was scored on a continuous basis.[3] The eyes were considered open if the cornea and pupil could be seen. Distinctions were not drawn among degrees of opening.

Heart Rate

Heart rate was entered into the computer every 10 sec by a scorer ignorant of infant condition or experimental treatment. The video portion of the tape was blacked out when this measure was coded.

All data were coded with the aid of an "observer" program (Noldus Information Technology Co., Wageningen, the Netherlands) that allows real-time data entry. The data were made available for statistical analysis via SYSTAT Version 5 (Systat, Inc., Evanston, IL).

STATISTICAL ANALYSIS

Each measure was evaluated in terms of the statistical significance of the experimental undertaking, initially through an analysis of variance (ANOVA) that featured a 2 (substance) × 2 (pacifier vs. sucrose) × 3 (baseline, treatment, posttreatment) repeated-measures design. Further evaluations were then undertaken through ANOVAs comparing water and sucrose across the 1-min treatment periods. This allowed us to determine

[3] Actually, this analysis was conducted at the suggestion of an anonymous reviewer of this *Monograph,* to whom we express our appreciation.

the operating characteristics of sucrose influence over the different coordinated behaviors and physiological systems studied here. The final statistical evaluation established regressions between activity changes, changes in crying, or hand-in-mouth behavior and heart rate.

For clarity of exposition, we first present the data for agitated infants, then those for calm infants. Within each state category, data are presented first for infants receiving fluids from a syringe and then for infants given a pacifier. Comparisons between syringe and pacifier delivery are made within each state. General data summaries of treatment effect, when warranted, are undertaken after all data have been presented and prior to the general discussion in Chapter V.

III. THE BEHAVIOR OF NORMAL NEWBORNS

THE BEHAVIOR OF NORMAL AGITATED NEWBORNS

The Effects of Sucrose Administered by Syringe

Baseline Profiles

There was very little variability in the behavior of agitated infants. They cried for a mean of 44.6 sec (± 4.5 sec SEM [standard error of the mean]) per minute during the 2 preceding min. Heart rate averaged 160.7 BPM (beats per minute) (± 6.6 BPM), and the mean activity score was 2.4 (± 0.19) during the 2-min qualifying interval. These were moderately upset infants who would have continued crying in the absence of intervention. According to our studies of infants born to methadone-maintained mothers (presented below) and of those born to cocaine-using mothers (E. M. Blass, V. Ciaramitaro, & A. J. Jain, unpublished observations, 1991), the normal agitated infants in the current study did not approach ceiling levels of distress as measured by crying, activity, or heart rate; the latter was often sustained in infants of drug-using mothers at upward of 200 BPM.

The Effects of Sucrose and Water on Crying

The overall analysis of variance (ANOVA) for crying that evaluated treatment (pacifier vs. syringe) and solution effects revealed a statistically significant effect of solution ($F[1, 28] = 15.36$, $p < .001$) but not of treatment ($F[1, 28] = 1.35$), with a significant interaction between treatment and solution ($F[1, 28] = 5.84$, $p < .02$). The meaning of the lack of pacifier effect and of the interaction will be discussed below. Figure 2 demonstrates that both sucrose and water effectively reduced the crying of agitated infants. Sucrose was especially effective—crying essentially stopped during the course of treatment. The lower levels of crying exhibited by those infants who received sucrose were maintained during the posttreatment pe-

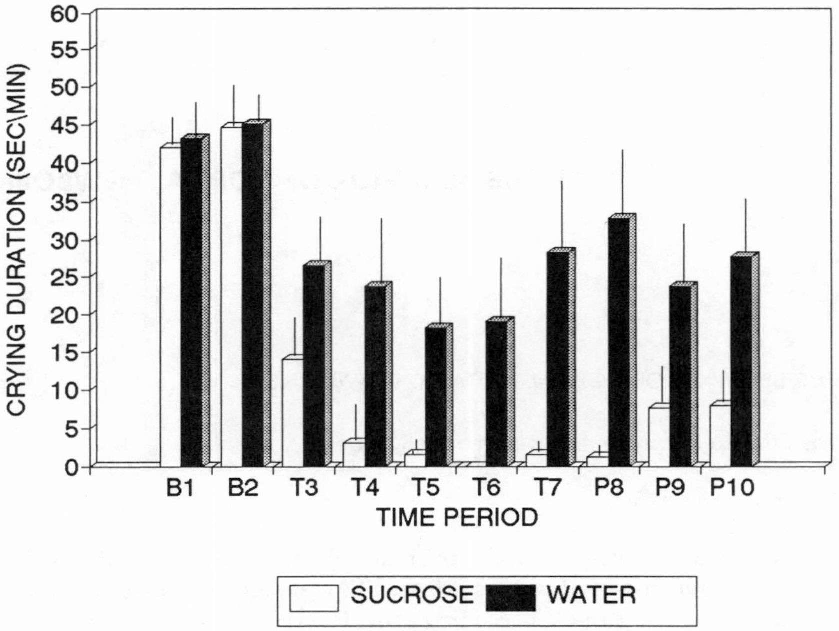

FIG. 2.—Mean (± S.E.) time (in seconds) spent crying each minute by agitated newborn humans who received either 0.1 ml of sucrose (open bars) once per minute or water (filled histograms) for 10 sec each minute. B1 and B2 refer to the first and second baseline minutes, respectively, preceding fluid delivery; T3–T7 refer to each of the 5-min fluid treatments; P8–P10 refer to each of the 3 posttreatment min that followed sucrose or water delivery. (The numbers refer to consecutive experimental minutes.)

riod; such was not the case, however, with those infants who received water, who continued to cry for 25–30 sec/min. Crying diminished rapidly in the sucrose group, falling to 14.05 sec during the first minute of treatment (i.e., after the infants had tasted only 0.1 ml of the 12% sucrose solution). An ANOVA showed a significant substance effect during both the treatment and the posttreatment periods ($F[1, 14] = 7.9$, $p < .01$, and $F[1, 14] = 10.2$, $p < .007$, respectively). There was no significant interaction.

Similarities and differences between present and past findings (Blass et al., 1989; Smith et al., 1990) concerning the effect of sucrose on crying are noteworthy. In both studies, sucrose was very effective, considerably more so than water. Even a 0.1-ml taste substantially reduced crying (note the T3 time frame in Fig. 2). Thus, we have replicated the basic phenomenon of sucrose taste markedly calming agitated, crying newborns, this time with infants drawn from a lower-SES population and tested in a hospital in which the patient-to-nurse ratio (12–15 : 1) was much higher than that (4 : 1) in the middle-class hospital in which our previous studies were conducted.

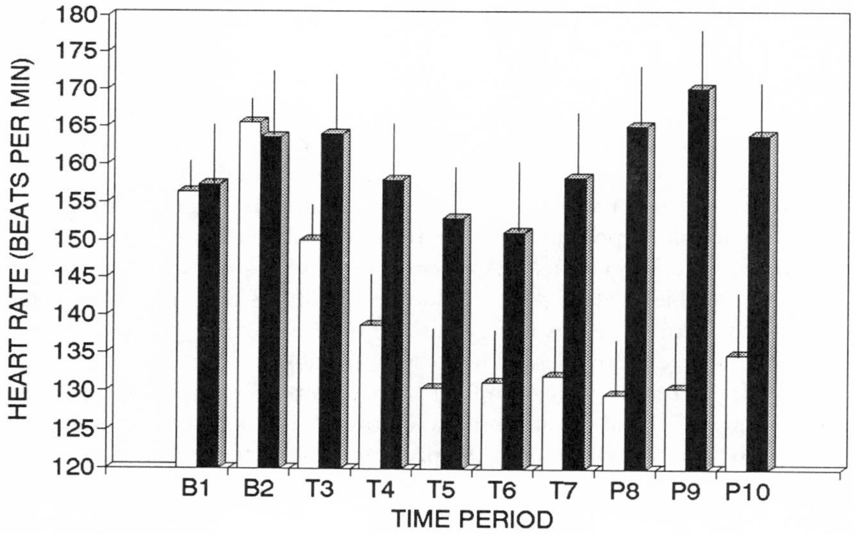

FIG. 3.—Mean (± S.E.) heart rate levels, expressed in beats per minute in infants who had received sucrose or water as per Fig. 2 above. Note the extreme protraction of bradycardia (P8–P10) in infants who received sucrose.

These data are also consistent with Barr's findings that a single 250 μl taste of sucrose calms newborn humans (Oberlander, Barr, Young, & Brian, 1992).

There are, however, two important differences between the pattern of results obtained in the previous and in the current studies. First, the calming effects in the current studies were not as enduring. Infants given sucrose cried a mean of 5.6 sec during each minute of the posttreatment period. Although this level of crying is substantially lower than baseline levels and far lower than that evinced by infants who received water, it is greater than previously reported. This increased incidence reflects a resumption of crying in five of the eight infants.

Second, in the present study, but not in our earlier ones, water was a relatively effective calming agent. Although water treatment somewhat reduced crying in our previous studies, the effect was very modest, was transient within the treatment period, and did not achieve statistical significance. The finding of a transient reduction in crying is replicated in the current study, but the reduction here is substantial—from 44.1 (± 4.3) to

21.9 ($\pm$ 8.1) sec—and was statistically significant in relation to the baseline level of crying ($p < .01$).

We do not see it as paradoxical that sucrose was relatively ineffective and water relatively effective in the two studies. Rather, we see these differences as stemming from a common origin, namely, the very high patient-to-nurse ratios in hospitals serving lower-SES areas. As dedicated as the team of nurses was, it was impossible for them to maintain a tight feeding and attention schedule, especially when there were problem infants in the nursery who required special care. As a result, because the nursery was kept at 72°F and the babies were tightly swaddled, the infants may have been relatively dehydrated as well as hungry at the time of testing. Viewed in this light, the relative effectiveness of water and the lack of extended quieting in infants given sucrose is understandable. The differences may have stemmed from minor procedural variations between the studies (e.g., different experimenters, the use of electrodes in the present study, or other possible subtle procedural differences), but we find these to be unlikely origins.

Heart Rate

As with crying, the overall ANOVA revealed a significant solution effect ($F[1, 28] = 8.17$, $p < .008$) and no pacifier effect (Fig. 3). Further analysis contrasting heart rate during and after treatment revealed no changes between treatment and posttreatment heart rate levels for solution or pacifier but a highly significant interaction between the two ($F[1, 28] = 8.29$, $p < .008$). This too will be discussed in the evaluation of pacifier effects on cardiac output. Sucrose caused an immediate reduction in heart rate that was sustained through the poststimulation period ($F[1, 14] = 12.2$, $p < .004$). This profound and sustained bradycardia in agitated infants was anticipated. First, as crying is reduced, fewer demands are placed on the cardiovascular system. Second, there is also a neuroanatomical basis for the reduction. The initial gustatory relay in the brain is the nucleus of the tractus solitarius (NTS), which actually consists of a group of nuclei in the brain stem that receive visceral (including taste) afferents (Lasiter, Wong, & Kachele, 1988). Transmission among these nuclei is mediated via opioid systems. One of the major efferent opioid systems involves NTS nuclei that determine cardiac output (Hassan, Feuerstein, & Faden, 1982). We will return to each of these themes.

Activity

According to the overall analysis of variance, there was a statistically significant effect of solution ($F[1, 28] = 3.96$, $p < .05$) and of pacifier

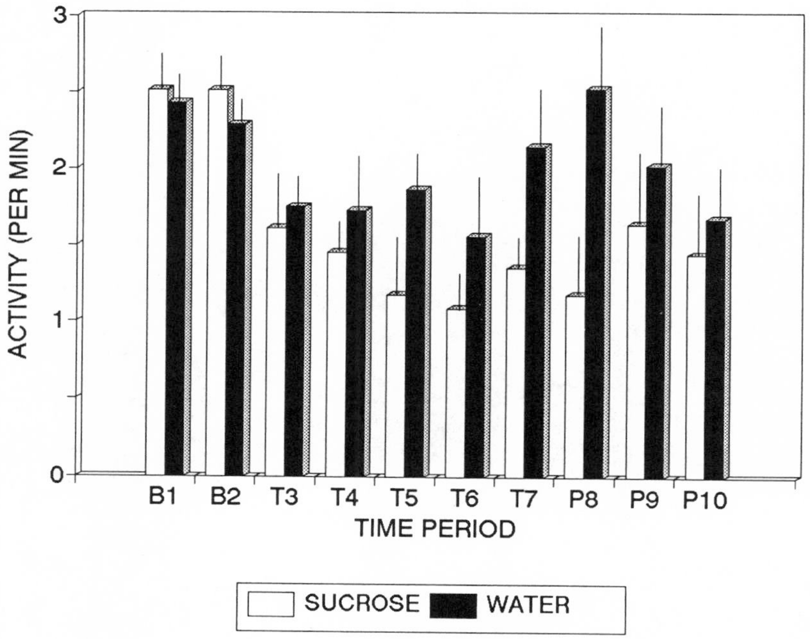

FIG. 4.—Mean (± S.E.) activity levels of agitated infants who received sucrose or water as described in Fig. 2 above. For details of the activity scale, see the text.

($F[1, 28] = 5.87$, $p < .02$) on activity. The interactions were not statistically significant. Sucrose reduced gross motor activity (Fig. 4). Activity dropped from a mean of 2.5 to a mean of 1.5 within 1 min of receiving 0.1 ml of the 12% sucrose solution and reached its nadir of 1.3 during the fourth minute of treatment. The effects of sucrose treatment on activity were most clearly revealed by a within-subjects repeated-measures ANOVA that compared the two before-treatment with the five treatment conditions ($F[6, 84] = 3.77$, $p < .002$). Activity fell linearly across treatment. According to Polynomial contrast, the linear component was statistically significant ($F[1, 14] = 16.946$, $p < .001$), and the interaction between the rate at which activity dropped and solution was also statistically significant ($F[1, 14] = 6.95$, $p < .02$).

The numbers belie the subjective effect of activity reduction. Shortly after being given one or two tastes of sucrose, these infants—whose extraordinary activity was in the form of short, rapid movements (a mean of 2.5 indicates vigorous movements of both arms, often from the shoulder and legs or head)—became calm. Their movements were more leisurely, generally consisting of the occasional movement of one arm toward the mouth. Leg and body activity had stopped. There was a certain amount of head

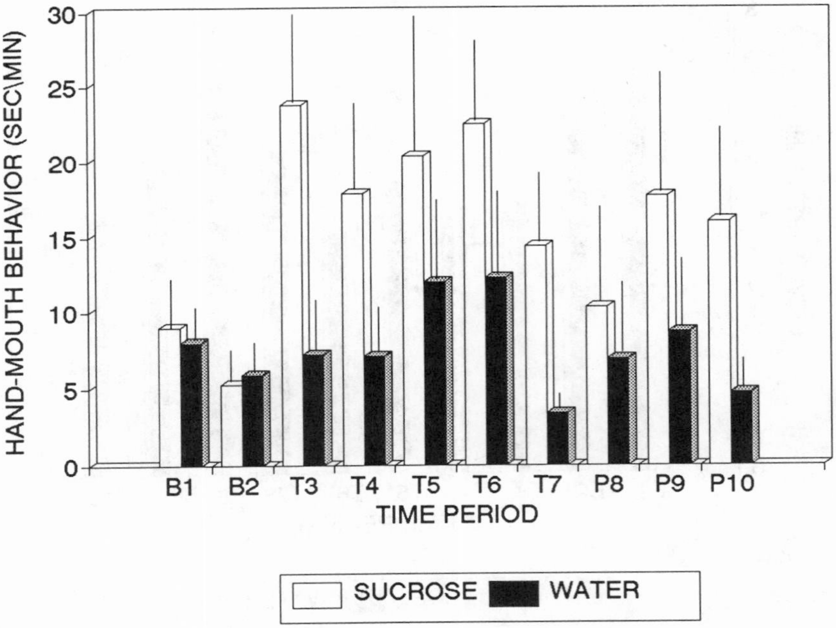

FIG. 5.—Mean (± S.E.) hand-mouth behavior expressed as seconds per minute in agitated human newborns before (B1–B2), during (T3–T7), and after (P8–P10) sucrose or water delivery.

movement, which was generally focused on capturing the hand as it either slid downward past the mouth or rested high up on the cheek. These head movements were determined by hand position. In the former case, the head tracked hand movement downward toward the chest; in the latter case, the head turned upward to catch the hand lodged on the zygomatic arch.

Water modulated activity less effectively than did sucrose, and the modest effect was transient as baseline was reattained during the fourth minute of water administration by syringe. If one accepts the idea that gross motor activity reflects the interaction between initial infant state and properties of the tastant, the lack of activity change in infants receiving water is not surprising. This is not paradoxical given water's effect on crying because infants' urgent thirst is alleviated through peripheral (oral) stimulation by water while change in activity reflects systemic events (as will be argued for sucrose-induced reductions), in particular, changes in central opioid release.

Hand-mouth behavior, which demands extraordinary coordination in newborns, emerged after crying had stopped and activity had been reduced (Fig. 5). Relative to baseline, it was sustained into the poststimulation period. Water delivery did not affect the likelihood of establishing and sustaining hand-mouth contact. Sucrose, however, did ($F[1, 14] = 5.5, p < .03$). In accord with our previously reported findings, a substantial increase in hand-mouth behavior occurred in all eight infants who received sucrose. The protraction of hand-mouth integration by infants who received sucrose supports the contention that bringing the hand to the mouth is an expression of a primitive feeding system that is engaged by sucrose taste.

It seems unlikely, however, that the hand in the mouth functions as a pacifier in the current situation because crying and hyperactivity had almost completely subsided before hand-mouth contact occurred. This emphasizes the multiple determination of this complex action system, its potential multiple functions in both calming and feeding, and the circumstances under which hand-mouth coordination occurs—this will be seen dramatically in methadone infants. The coordination of hand and mouth in newborns may be a starting point in the development of motor and motivational representations of action. Through its ability to manipulate breast and nipple to obtain milk, the mouth discovers tactile properties of objects that are unavailable to the visual system. In addition to its other functions, bringing the hand to the mouth may prepare the infant for future exploration of objects with the mouth.

Relations among Different Measures

Two relations of note are that between the cessation of crying/the reduction of activity and the initiation of hand-mouth behavior and that between change in activity and change in heart rate.

The relation between crying and hand-mouth behavior can be documented as follows. Six of the eight infants who brought their hands to their mouths had already stopped crying and did not resume crying during sucrose treatment even after they removed their hands from their mouths. The hand was not instrumental in maintaining calm because neither activity nor crying levels during the poststimulation period were related to duration of hand-mouth activity. (A different profile will be presented for the infants of methadone-maintained mothers.) The occurrence of this coordinated action has at least two interpretations. One is that the taste of sucrose engaged a feeding system and that bringing the hand to the mouth is a manifestation of this nascent system. Alternatively, hand-to-mouth behavior may be part of a well-coordinated action system that simply requires the right level of activation for its expression. Very quiet infants with low activity levels do not manifest hand-in-mouth behavior because of lack of movement; agitated infants' activity exceeds the limits of coordination necessary for the moving hand and the moving head to establish and maintain linkage.

The relation between heart rate (HR) and activity (*a*) is noteworthy.

The decline in heart rate did not correlate with the decline in crying, which was precipitous, or with hand-mouth behavior, which remained stable during the test period. Moreover, a decline in heart rate always preceded the onset of hand-mouth behavior. The relations between activity and heart rate are captured by Figure 6. During the baseline period, the relation is essentially flat and is expressed formally by the regression $HR = 4a + 170$. The relation changes markedly during and after stimulation, however, especially in infants who received sucrose, which reduced both activity and heart rate. These reductions extended into the poststimulation period. These changes are expressed formally as $HR = 17.1a + 126.0$ and $HR = 14.0a + 136.3$ during and after sucrose and water treatment, respectively.

Although activity influenced heart rate, its influence accounts only partially for the marked reduction because heart rate continued to decline well after activity levels had stabilized. A fuller understanding comes from a consideration of the anatomical and functional relation between gustatory-visceral afferent projections and cardiac control. As indicated, the NTS is the site of the first gustatory synapse. The NTS also contains the integrative system for cardiac function. Thus, within the NTS and the medulla (Punnen & Sapru, 1986), gustatory and ingestive afferents are linked through opioid mediation to determine cardiac rate and output. It thus seems likely that taste-induced engagement of cardiac control within the NTS also contributed to the normalization of the heart rate, independent of changes in gross activity.

In short, the major findings of this aspect of the study are consonant with the idea that opioids in newborn humans, and perhaps in other species, manage energy conservation. In particular, considerably less energy is expended when crying ceases and when activity is reduced. Cardiovascular output is likewise reduced, as is oxygen consumption.[4] Finally, to the extent that our interpretation of hand-mouth involvement is valid, then a feeding system underlying energy repletion is also engaged. Note that all these changes occur within 1 min of the delivery of 0.1 ml of sucrose (but, according to our 30-sec measures, not immediately) and that they endure. The orchestration of energy-conserving-and-repleting behavioral and physiological alterations initiated by sucrose, the enduring nature of the changes, and the fact that such changes are frequently iterated daily through mother-infant reunions makes taste-induced, central opioid changes likely participants in neonatal learning. Understanding the occurrence and the consequences of these central changes may provide insights into the development of the motivation systems that underlie the mother-infant relationship.

[4] Recently, using direct calorimetry, Rao, Blass, Brignol, Marino, and Glass (1993) have discovered that 0.1–0.2 ml of sucrose cause a 10% reduction (range 7%–17%) in energy expenditure in crying infants. The drop occurred in 100% of the tests ($N = 10$).

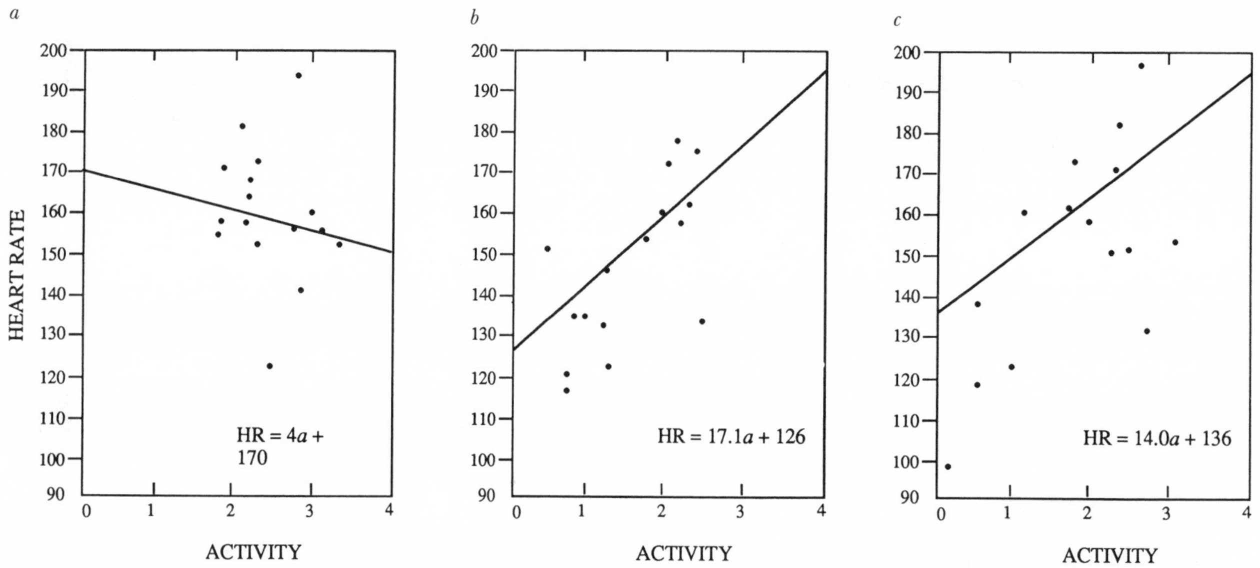

FIG. 6.—Correlation between gross activity and heart rate before (Fig. 6*a*), during (Fig. 6*b*), and after (Fig. 6*c*) sucrose or water treatment. Each data point represents the confluence of the mean activity and heart rate scores per minute for each minute for each subject.

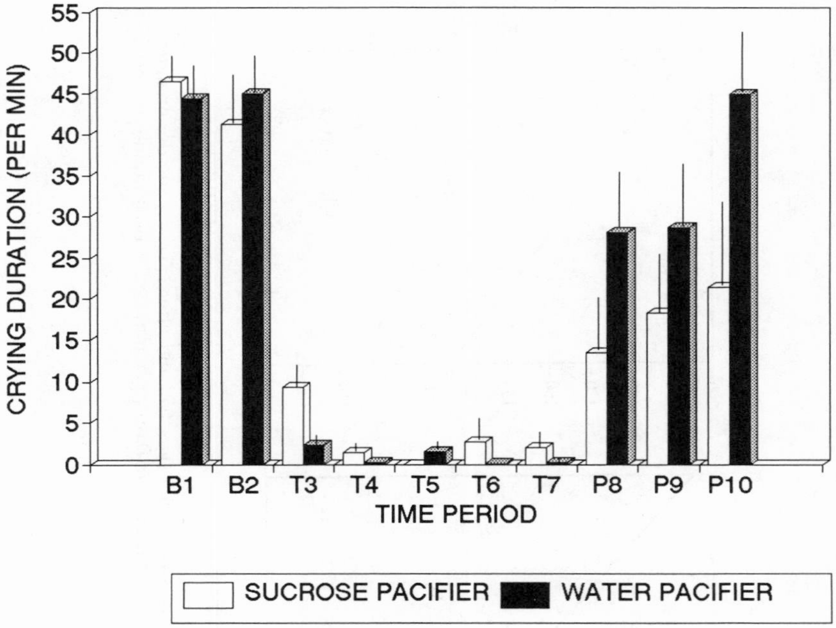

FIG. 7.—Mean (± S.E.) amount of time (seconds per minute) spent crying before (B1–B2), during (T1–T7), and after (P8–P10) treatment with pacifiers that were coated with either sucrose or water. Note the rapidity of crying decline and return on pacifier application and removal, especially in the water-pacifier condition (N = 8 subjects per condition).

These issues will be addressed at length in the general discussion in Chapter V.

The Effects of Pacifiers

Crying

As indicated earlier, the overall between-groups ANOVA did not yield a statistically significant pacifier effect for crying but did result in a statistically significant interaction between solution and pacifier effects. This interaction can be appreciated from the poststimulation portion of Figure 7, which demonstrates that infants whose pacifier had been coated with sucrose cried less after the pacifier was removed than infants who had sucked a water-coated pacifier. A between-subjects repeated-measures ANOVA of the pacifier data (baseline vs. treatment) revealed a significant pacifier effect ($F[1, 14] = 12.483$, $p < .001$) but not a significant solution effect.

Pacifier stimulation caused changes that were both similar to and different from those caused by sucrose stimulation alone (cf. Figs. 2 and 7). In both instances, crying stopped. In the case of pacifier stimulation, cessation was instantaneous regardless of the substance administered, whereas, in the case of sucrose stimulation alone, cessation was virtually complete for the group only by the third delivery of sucrose. This difference probably reflects the continuous and active stimulation produced by the pacifier and its vigorous engagement of the sucking response. Sucrose taste alone does not elicit sucking, although it does cause the baby to make licking and savoring movements, such as, for example, lip smacking.

Second, infants began crying again when the pacifier was removed in both pacifier conditions, especially those infants whose pacifier had been coated with water; baseline levels of crying in the latter were reattained within the third minute after pacifier removal. This was reflected in the overall ANOVA (as indicated above) and allows us to focus on the specific contrast effect of solution during posttreatment in infants who received a pacifier. According to ANOVA, the differences in crying between infants who received water and those who received sucrose on their pacifier approached statistical significance ($F[1, 14] = 3.81$, $p < .06$). For pacifier-sucrose infants, the rebound after removal was more modest, reaching 50% of baseline levels. The resumption of crying at baseline levels by the pacifier-water infants after pacifier removal suggests, first, that stimulation of the oral cavity with a pacifier quiets but does not cause a fundamental state change (on this point, see also Smith et al., 1990). Second, the period of quiescence may have provided sufficient rest to allow additional energy expenditure to reflect the infant's agitated state. Thus, pacifier taste also influenced behavior; agitated infants can process both orotactile and orogustatory (i.e., sweet taste) information during suckling. These pathways may naturally combine to produce rapid and sustained calming in newborns.

Heart Rate

Figure 8 demonstrates that the presence of a pacifier also reduced heart rate markedly ($F[6, 84] = 8.97$, $p < .0001$). As expected, for both sucrose- and water-coated pacifiers, the decline was gradual, achieving asymptote of circa 130 BPM during the third minute of treatment (Polynomial $F[1, 14] = 5.57$, $p < .03$). Pacifier solution did not affect heart rate during treatment. Thus, changes in heart rate can be dissociated from those in crying and activity (discussed below), which dropped to asymptote levels instantaneously during pacifier stimulation. The organizations of crying, activity, and heart rate obviously differ, each having different demand characteris-

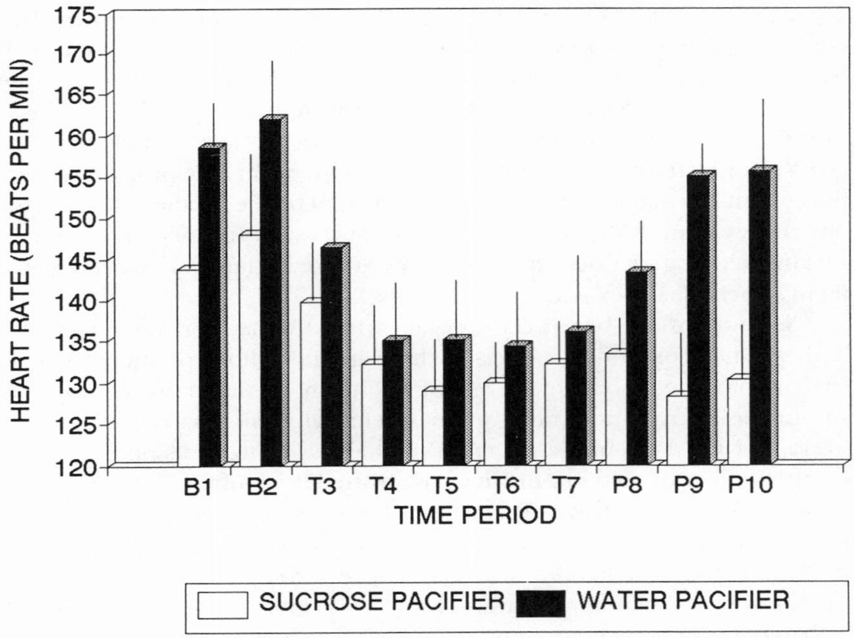

FIG. 8.—Mean (± S.E.) heart rate levels expressed in beats per minute in newborns who sucked sucrose- or water-coated pacifiers during the treatment period. Note the rapid reversal of heart rate on water-pacifier removal and the stability of bradycardia in pacifier-sucrose infants.

tics, controls, and underlying structures. That is the point. Each system reflects a perturbation through its own response characteristics and determinants—only some of which are shared. Moreover, each system responds differently to different classes of proximal stimulation—in these particular instances, sucrose and pacifier.

Differences between the influence of water and that of sucrose on the newborn are highlighted in the change in cardiac output after the pacifier was removed ($F[1, 14] = 7.45$, $p < .02$). The heart rate of those infants given a sucrose-coated pacifier essentially did not waver after the pacifier was removed from the mouth. In contrast, the heart rate of those infants given a water-coated pacifier accelerated rapidly after the pacifier was removed. This differential response of heart rate to pacifier removal leads us to focus on the actual exchanges between mother and infant during normal nursing-suckling engagements and on the enduring physiological, gastric, central, and behavioral consequences and sequelae of the exchanges. During the normal course of events, the nipple/breast causes the major, immediate calming/normalizing effects on the infant; these effects endure because

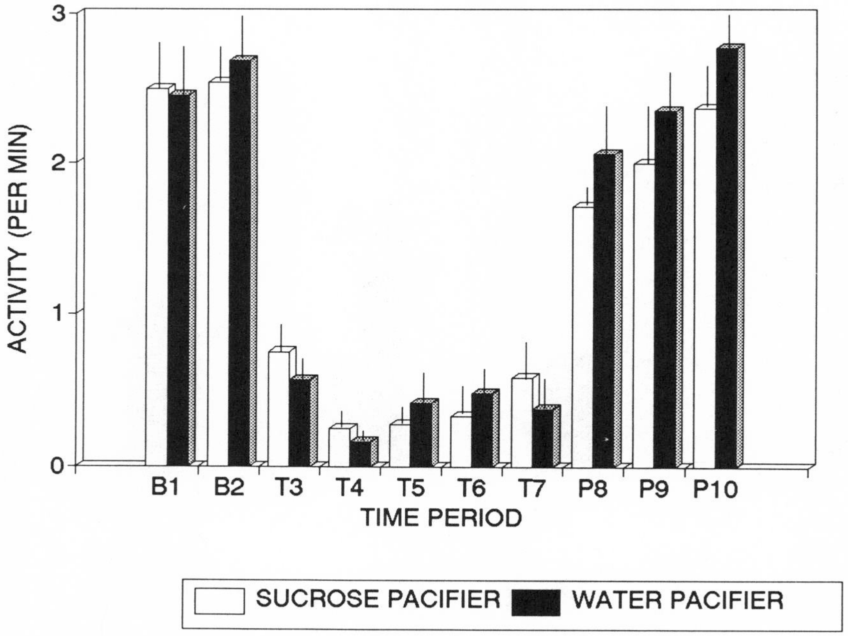

FIG. 9.—Mean (± S.E.) activity levels (see the text) for the infants presented in Fig. 7 above. Activity essentially ceased within the first minute of treatment. Both pacifier-sucrose and pacifier-water infants remained quiescent throughout treatment but resumed baseline levels of activity as soon as the pacifier was removed.

of the central changes induced by the flavor of the milk and possible postingestive effects.

Activity

The activity pattern (presented in Fig. 9) shows important similarities to and differences from the profile of change in crying following sucrose administration. In particular, activity came to an immediate halt that persisted as long as the pacifier remained in the mouth ($F[6, 84] = 3.498, p < .001$). There were no significant differences in activity between pacifier groups. Substance effects, moreover, were not manifest when the pacifier was removed. The activity levels of infants given sucrose and water increased at the same rate, and both groups reached the same asymptote. Thus, changes in general activity were not enduring; whether the infants received a pacifier dipped in sucrose or water, their activity was controlled by pacifier stimulation alone and did not reflect a fundamental state change.

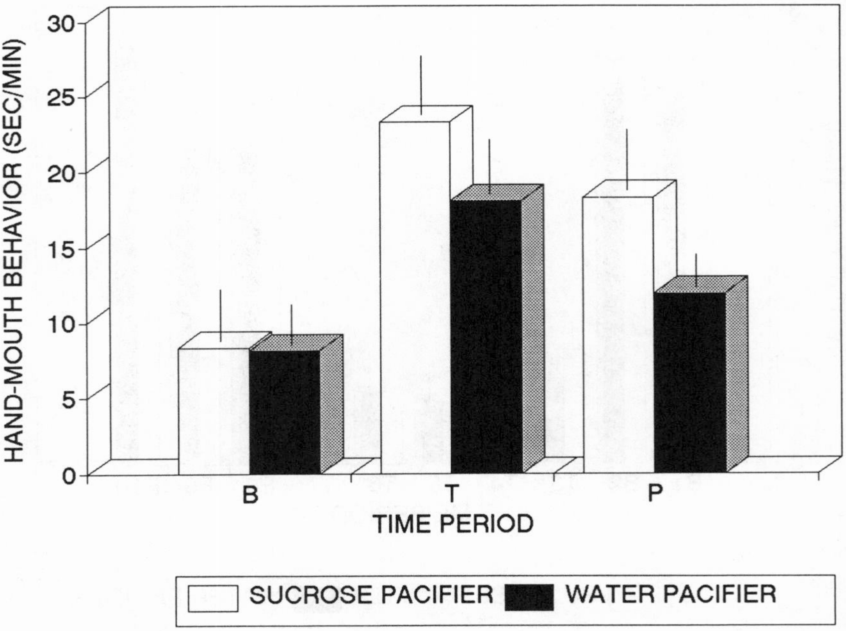

FIG. 10.—Mean (± S.E.) amount of time (seconds per minute) during which hand-mouth behavior was exhibited each minute before (B), during (T), and after (P) pacifier-water or pacifier-sucrose treatment.

Hand-Mouth Coordination

The effects of pacifier insertion on hand-mouth coordination are captured in Figure 10. Presence of the pacifier alone very effectively brought the infants' hands to their mouths ($F[1, 14] = 6.501$, $p < .02$). When the pacifier was removed, this effect was reversed immediately in the pacifier-water group and within 3 min in the pacifier-sucrose group. It is interesting that the effects of sucrose alone and of pacifier alone were not additive in infants who received pacifier-sucrose stimulation. The protraction of hand-mouth behavior in infants who received a sucrose-coated pacifier ($F[1, 14] = 2.7$, $p < .06$) demonstrates that state changes caused by sucrose taste endured after the pacifier was removed.

Eye Opening

Figure 11 presents the percentage of time that agitated infants kept their eyes open before, during, and after their respective treatments. Al-

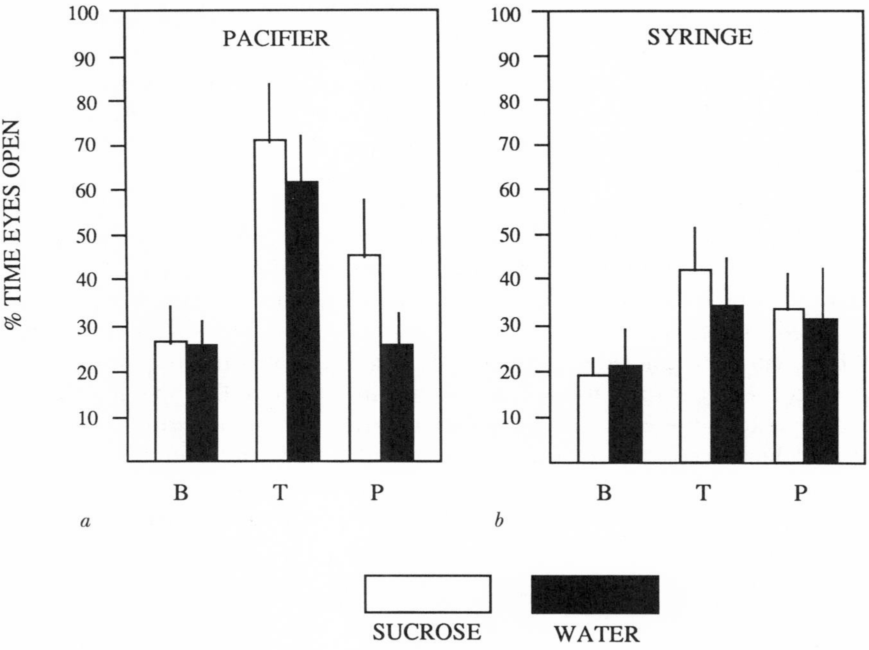

FIG. 11.—Percentage of time that agitated newborn infants kept their eyes open before (B), during (T), and after (P) treatment with a pacifier (Fig. 11*a*) or a syringe (Fig. 11*b*). Infants who received sucrose are represented by open histograms, those who received water by filled histograms.

though the pattern of findings is consistent with those obtained for the other measures in this study, there are also revealing differences. Infants' reactions to the pacifier are absolutely consistent with their reactions to the other measures. The infants' eyes were open 71% and 62% of the time while sucking on sucrose- and water-coated pacifiers, respectively ($F[1, 14] = 11.168$, $p < .002$), relative to baseline. The difference between substances was not statistically significant during treatment. As with the other measures, removal of the pacifier changed the level of eye opening ($F[1, 14] = 22.15$, $p < .001$). During the poststimulation period, infants who had sucked a sucrose-coated pacifier kept their eyes open somewhat longer relative to baseline eye opening, although the differences between sucrose and water were not statistically significant. Agitated infants who received fluid by syringe spent almost twice as long with their eyes open. Again, there were no differences between the effect of sucrose and water on eye opening during or after treatment. There was no decline between the treatment and the posttreatment phase regardless of the solution delivered. This lack of change cannot be attributed to ceiling or basement effects or to whether infants resumed crying. The pacifier data demonstrate that eye-opening controls were not invariant and, like all other measures in this study, could be driven by the synergy of infant state and local stimulation. The marked elevation in eye opening (62%–71%) was well above the baseline levels of calm infants (as will be shown below), suggesting a direct control between orogustatory stimulation and eye opening.

This segment of the study, therefore, has demonstrated that eye opening can be brought under the control of orotactile stimulation. We have not provided direct evidence of taste affecting eye opening because infants who received sucrose alone did not differ from those who received water alone. We interpret protracted eye opening during the treatment phase within the perspective of the formation of the mother-infant bond. Eye opening within the context of the changes documented above becomes integral to the system of facial recognition. Indeed, 3-day-old infants preferentially look at their own mother's face over that of a woman of similar lactational status matched experimentally for facial and complexion features (Bushnell et al., 1983).

Discussion

These two sets of experiments on agitated human newborns support the conclusion that two different central systems interdependently orchestrate behavioral and physiological effectors involved in state change, energy conservation, and growth. Each system is potent in its own right. Each system mediating gustatory taste, texture, and pressure can independently reverse state in agitated infants who are crying up to 60%–75% of the time. It is of considerable interest that, for hand-mouth contact and eye opening, the two behaviors for which there was neither a basement effect nor intrinsic constraints on rate of change (as in heart rate), there was no additivity between taste and texture afferents, suggesting competition in the final pathways shared by the two central systems.

Even at the current level of analysis, there are two major differences between tactile and gustatory systems that shed light on their natural functioning during nursing-suckling interactions. The time parameters of change differ in important ways. Both crying and activity essentially stop when a pacifier is placed in the mouth. This abrupt change presumably reflects direct neural mediation of tactile stimulation or of the sucking that that stimulation elicits. After administration of sucrose, the most potent taste stimulus that we have studied, it takes about 2 min for crying to stop completely, and activity decreases slowly (recall the linear effect established by ANOVA), reaching an asymptote that is higher than that achieved almost instantaneously with the plain pacifier. Second, in keeping with the more protracted contribution of opioid mediation, the effects of sucrose on crying, heart rate, and hand-mouth behavior in agitated infants are longer lasting than pacifier effects. It is of considerable interest in this regard that crying during blood collection via heel prick for PKU (phenylketonuria) evaluation was most effectively reduced by imposing a 2-min delay between tasting sucrose (2 ml) and the onset of blood collection (Blass, 1993). This suggests a consolidation time for opioid effectiveness. The pacifier, of course, works immediately in combating pain.

We will elaborate on this in the general discussion in Chapter V. For the present, we propose a dual mechanism of action underlying normal suckling, energy enhancement, and energy conservation in agitated infants. Contact with the mother—especially suckling contact that stimulates the massive projections of the trigeminal nerves—reorients the infant's behavior toward the mouth, significantly reducing or excluding the influence of other sources of stimulation. After suckling, orotactile control over state, metabolic change, and energy conservation is transferred to the gustatory system, reflecting the effect of milk's taste; still later, control is transferred to postabsorptive events, ultimately leading to sleep (Antin, Gibbs, Holt, Young, & Smith, 1975). The transition from alimentary station to station, therefore, prolongs energy-conserving characteristics induced by suckling even in the absence of the initial, powerful proximal stimulus provided by contact with the mother and the oral stimulation afforded by breast, nipple, and taste.

These particular findings are predicted only by a model that asserts that the pacifier is acting through a neural on-off system that remains effective only as long as the pacifier stimulates the mouth and the infant actively suckles. The model also asserts that sucrose engages an opioid system that remains active after the cessation of the proximal gustatory stimulus, its dilution by saliva, other tastes, or adaptation. These properties are presented at the level of the mouth in Figure 12.

The model starts with the mother (M) approaching and nursing her infant. Through this one act, she affects the infant's behavior through at least two pathways, each with different operating characteristics. The tactile qualities of breast and nipple affect behavior through a nonopioid pathway in an on-off fashion. Taste (flavor) casts its influence through opioid pathways in a "ramp" fashion characterized by a slower rate of onset and a more protracted effective period after stimulus offset. The one exception to this is pacifier effects on heart rate, which cause a gradual decline even though both crying and activity drop precipitously. This reflects the intrinsic organization of cardiac function that protects against rapid sustained fluctuations in cardiac output and blood pressure.

Other models concerning sucrose and/or pacifier actions make very

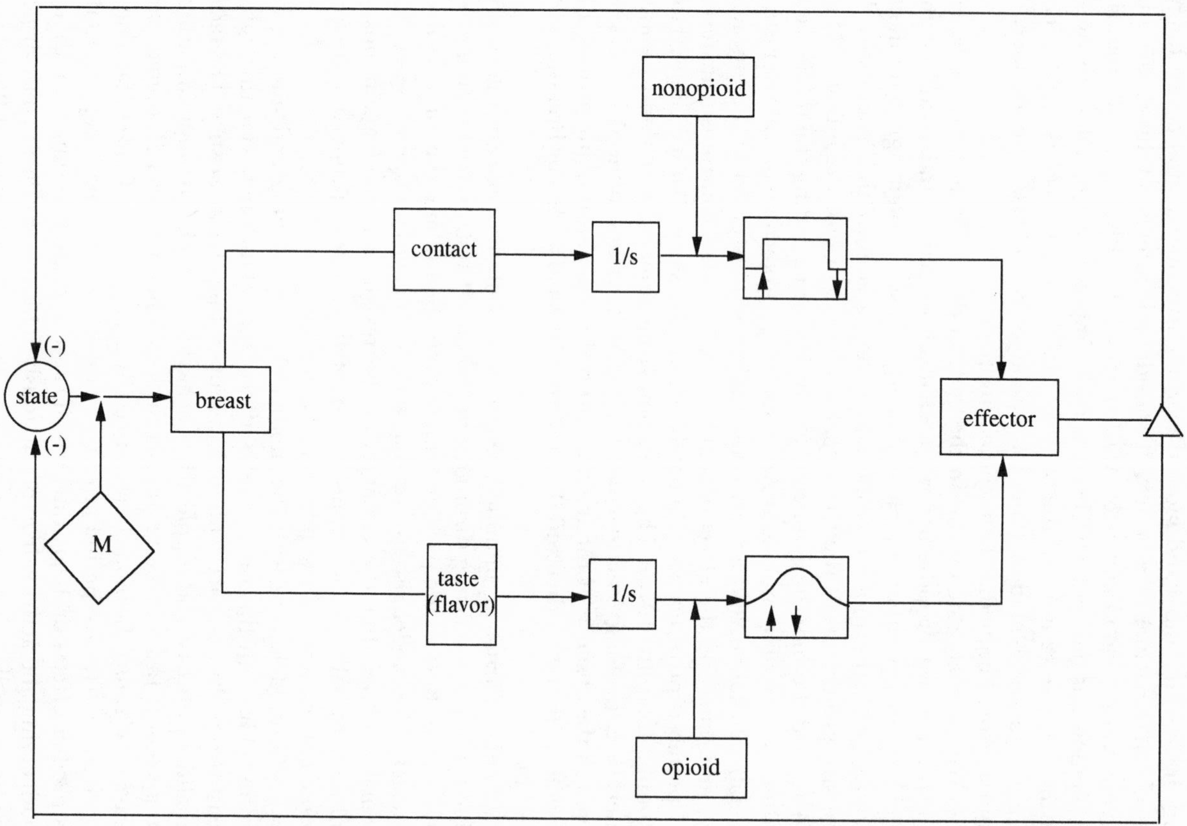
state
(-)
(-)
M
breast
contact
taste
(flavor)
1/s
1/s
nonopioid
opioid
effector

different predictions. Behavioral models based on contrast alone predict that infants will start to cry immediately on termination of either form of stimulation. Models based on habituation predict that the calming effects of either sucrose or pacifier will be relatively brief. A habituation model may be appropriate for a study of the behavior of infants receiving water alone, where all effects except crying are reversed within 1–2 min of the termination of stimulation. The parallel changes in all measures at the termination of sucrose administration and the different set of parallel changes on pacifier removal make it more likely that common adjustments are governed by a central mediator for each system that determines the operations of each output. As indicated, the data generally argue against additivity.

Infants seize the opportunity to associate a particular figure and her features with these changes and to change their emotional disposition toward this figure. The short-term changes described here are not sleep inducing. This is particularly true for pacifier stimulation, which invariably induced eye opening in agitated infants. The calm induced by pacifier and sucrose with its attendant eye opening, therefore, can provide an ideal state and affective context for infants to learn about the particular features of their mothers. A number of studies have demonstrated that this capacity is present in the olfactory (Macfarlane, 1975; Porter & Moore, 1981; Schaal, 1988), tactile (Blass et al., 1984; Sullivan et al., 1991), auditory (Blass, 1990), and visual (Bushnell et al., 1983) domains in newborns. Eye opening in response to the presence of a pacifier and during periods when babies are alert and calm may be functional. The mother's face is preferred to that of a stranger by 3-day-old infants (Bushnell et al., 1983) and her odor over that of a woman of similar lactational status by 6-day-olds.

FIG. 12.—Model specifying the mechanisms that underlie the changes in infant behavior and physiology that occur during nursing. These changes are induced at the level of the mouth and do not reflect the postingestive consequences of suckling. For the sake of exposition, the infant, starting in an agitated state, is picked up by the mother (M) and suckles her breast. Suckling causes two changes. One is mediated by contact, i.e., through pressure and tactile detectors that are part of the trigeminal nerve complex. The physical characteristics of nipple and breast are transduced (1/s, i.e., transduction from peripheral to central change) through nonopioid neural systems that operate in an on-off manner, as shown by the rectangular representation. The behavioral (crying, activity, hand-mouth) and physiological effector systems are thus influenced by the output of the central systems and in turn cause changes in infant state. Milk taste (or flavor) is detected in the mouth and transduced via opioid systems in the base of the brain in a graded manner, with slower onset and offset times relative to the contact systems. The same classes of effectors are influenced through pathways that are anatomically or pharmacologically separable at some point. These changes too influence infant state as measured in the current studies. The overall system is one of negative feedback but with an open loop because state changes (except as constrained by the immobility of sleep) do not influence the likelihood of sucking.

THE BEHAVIOR OF NORMAL CALM NEWBORNS

The Effects of Sucrose

In all, 32 calm infants (eight each receiving water or sucrose delivered by syringe or pacifier) were studied. Infants were designated as calm if they cried less than 24 sec/min during the 10 min that preceded stimulation and were in an alert state as judged by eye opening and gross motor activity scores of approximately 0.5 or more.

Results

By the end of the 10-min qualification period (i.e., the last 2 min), the infants were at rest and did not cry. Except for occasional arm movements, they were essentially inactive (activity = 0.6). No incidents of hand-mouth behavior exceeded 1–2 sec. Baseline heart rate was stable at 144 BPM for the sucrose group and 127 BPM for the water group.

Calm infants who received sucrose never cried. And, while three infants who received water did begin to cry, the crying was not sustained. In terms of both the incidence of crying and its duration, this induction accords well with our experiences with nondeprived, nondehydrated newborn and older infants who received water by syringe. Aversive reactions to water are also seen in rats, which are vulnerable to water intoxication brought on by continued drinking (Blass & Hall, 1976; Hall & Blass, 1975). This issue of water aversion will be addressed in the general discussion in Chapter V, in which we evaluate the physiological consequences of ingestion.

None of the calm infants who received sucrose brought their hands to their mouths. This exemplifies in human infants a principle that has recently been well established in infant rats: relatively high levels of activity must provide a background against which specific peripheral and central stimulation can gain control over complex motor patterns (Hall, 1979; Moran, Lew, & Blass, 1981). Activity levels were low to start with and continued essentially without change. Thus, sucrose does not necessarily reduce ongoing levels of general activity in human newborns. Rather, it drives activity toward the basal level of a quiet alert state. (We may have been stymied here, of course, by basement effects.)

The effects of sucrose and pacification on heart rate changes in calm infants indicate how state determines the pathway that will be utilized to alter cardiac output. Whereas the administration of sucrose and the presence of a pacifier each reduced heart rate in agitated infants, only sucrose did so in calm infants ($F[1, 28] = 3.31, p < .05$), and the difference between baseline and treatment pacifier conditions was statistically significant only when the pacifier had been treated with sucrose (note the flat function for pacifier-water in the filled histograms in the lower portion of Fig. 13). In both sucrose alone and sucrose-pacifier, the differences between treatment and posttreatment effects did not change, suggesting an enduring effect of treatment. Finally, the pacifier appears to facilitate sucrose's effect on heart rate in these calm infants; whereas sucrose alone caused a reduction of circa 10 BPM and the pacifier alone was essentially ineffectual, the combination caused a sustained reduction of circa 15 BPM.

Eye opening.—During baseline periods, calm infants kept their eyes open 42% of the time on average. Eye opening was not affected by either insertion of the pacifier or tasting water or sucrose ($p > .10$), nor did it change during the poststimulation period. This again demonstrates that the effectiveness of a manipulation depends on the infant's state. Calm, alert infants simply did not open their eyes more frequently or for longer durations under any of the stimulus conditions of this experiment. Thus, the pacifier's effectiveness in causing eye opening in agitated infants depended on the infant moving from a state of high arousal to one of calm while receiving orotactile stimulation. Accordingly, the likelihood of an act occurring in newborn humans reflects (*a*) the infant's state, (*b*) how it came to that state, (*c*) the rate at which the state was attained, and (*d*) the proximate stimulation. For eye opening to be sustained, the infant must be in a calm state but must have reached that state as a result of pacifier stimulation. Neither calm alone nor calm with either pacifier stimulation or sucrose stimulation was sufficient. State change alone is not sufficient because sucrose alone was not effective in agitated infants.

Discussion

In important ways, the behavior of calm newborns receiving sucrose or a pacifier serves as a foil to that of agitated newborns treated identically. The contrast highlights the multiple determinants of behavior, even in newborns. Calm infants could have reduced their activity in response to the presence of sucrose or a pacifier alone, yet they did not. Heart rate decelerated only by about 10–15 BPM. Infants did not bring their hands to their mouths, and rooting was difficult to elicit. Eye opening was not enhanced. These findings speak to cyclicity (i.e., intrinsic rhythms affecting responsivity) in infant behavior at birth and to the differential availability of entire behavioral patterns to external influences.

Mechanism of action.—As indicated earlier, parallel studies of infant rats have yielded results that are harmonious with those of studies of human newborns. In particular, sucrose (other sugars, milk, and fat) reduces vocalization in isolated infant rats and markedly increases the pain threshold. The same holds for suckling a nonlactating nipple (Blass et al., 1990; Blass,

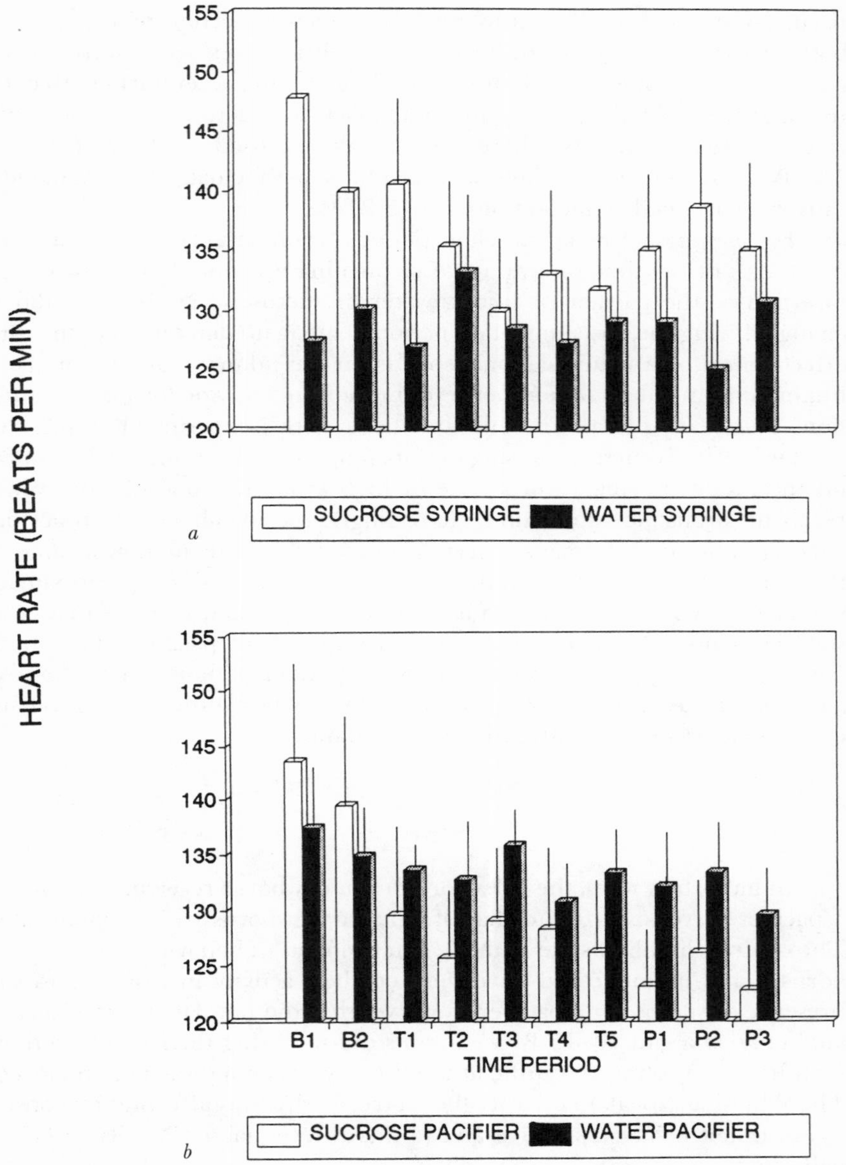

FIG. 13.—Mean (± S.E.) heart rate of calm newborn humans who received either sucrose or water via a syringe (Fig. 13*a*) or a pacifier (Fig. 13*b*).

Shide, Zaw-Mon, & Sorentino, 1993). The time parameters exhibited by rats parallel those exhibited by human infants. There is rapid onset and rapid offset for nipple sucking per se and more leisurely onset and more protracted offset for sugar, milk, or fat stimulation. The rat studies have also implicated the endogenous opioids in sucrose mediation and have strongly suggested that contact comforting is not opioid mediated. Let us briefly summarize this evidence because it bears directly on the next study, one of infants born to methadone-maintained mothers.

First, rats that receive intraoral infusions of sucrose or certain other substances behave just like rats injected with morphine systemically (Kehoe & Blass, 1986a, 1986b) or, in microgram quantities, directly into the brain (Kehoe & Blass, 1986c). Their vocalization is markedly reduced, and they are better able to withstand noxious stimulation. Second, drugs that antagonize the action of morphine at their receptor reverse the calming effects of both systemic and central morphine injections and milk, sucrose, and fat infusions into the mouth (Blass & Fitzgerald, 1988; Blass et al., 1987; Kehoe & Blass, 1986a; Shide & Blass, 1989). These antagonists, such as naloxone and naltrexone, also attenuate the pain-reducing effects of morphine injections and sucrose, fat, and milk infusions. Third, the quieting and pain relief caused by the mother and suckling contact per se are not affected by doses of naloxone that fully reverse the calming effects of a moderate dose of morphine (Blass, Fillion, Weller, & Brunson, 1990; Blass et al., 1993). In this regard, the drug beta-FNA, a selective mμ receptor toxin, prevents morphine but not contact from being effective in rats (Winslow & Insel, 1990).

IV. THE BEHAVIOR OF INFANTS BORN TO METHADONE-MAINTAINED WOMEN

The striking behavioral parallels between rat and human newborns encourage a search for common mechanisms. For obvious ethical and medical reasons, one cannot inject human infants with opioid antagonists. The availability of drugs in contemporary society makes it possible, however, to study newborn human infants whose mothers were maintained on methadone during pregnancy. (For other reasons, we have also studied infants whose mothers used cocaine during pregnancy. These studies will be reported separately.)

The predictions are clear cut. If opioid systems normally contribute to calm, then "methadone infants" should be extremely agitated during their withdrawal phase. This is predicated on the fact that, in response to chronically elevated methadone levels, endogenous opioids are markedly reduced (negative feedback from occupied receptors shuts down opioid synthesis) and recover slowly to base levels during withdrawal. It follows that sucrose should not affect the agitation experienced by methadone infants because gustatory afferents cannot cause opioid release in infants whose levels of endogenous opioids are very low to start with. Yet a pacifier should effectively soothe these infants because central nonopioid pathways should be available for calming.

These studies were also conducted in Jamaica Hospital, Queens, New York. Heroin at present is not the drug of choice on the street; cocaine is. There are relatively few people in methadone treatment (in fact, methadone centers are being closed nationally). Consequently, we have studied intermittently only four infants born to methadone-maintained mothers. Because the data were so consistent among these four and are so germane to the other work described in this *Monograph,* we present them here in preliminary form as we collect additional data for a more comprehensive report.

SUBJECTS

One infant was an African-American male, the second a Caucasian female, the third a Hispanic female, and the fourth an African-American female. The first and third infants were cared for by their mothers daily in the hospital; the second and fourth were put up for adoption. All four infants were born at term, and their mean weight was 3,398 grams. Their Apgar scores ranged from 7 to 9 at 1 min and from 8 to 10 at 5 min after birth.

Standard treatment for methadone infants was followed by hospital staff: when withdrawal symptoms (e.g., excessive crying and irritability) were first observed, the infants were tightly swaddled and efforts made to keep a pacifier in their mouth. In order to calm them and reduce crying and hyperactivity, these infants were given phenobarbital; dosages started at 7.0–7.5 mg twice daily and gradually tapered off to zero over the course of 3–4 weeks. To help relieve constipation, 5 drops of paregoric (which contains 0.04% morphine) were administered every 6 hours daily. This too was gradually reduced to naught during the course of treatment. All infants were bottle fed by staff, with the mothers providing two of the meals daily for the two infants indicated above.

Because so few infants born to methadone-maintained mothers were available for study, the four in our sample were utilized as much as possible, with a number of manipulations being performed across a session. In our studies, we sought to establish whether sucrose can reduce agitation, whether it can prevent agitation, whether a pacifier can prevent agitation, and whether a pacifier can maintain calm in methadone infants.

On the basis of the rat studies, we predicted that sucrose would not calm these infants but that the pacifier would because its effects are mediated through pathways that do not depend on opioid systems. To assess the effects of either sucrose or a pacifier (or both) on the various measures utilized here, treatment was initiated either after a 30-sec baseline period of intense crying or after the infant's heart rate had reached a level of 215 BPM, whichever came first. Treatment consisted of 0.5 ml of 18% sucrose administered every 30 sec.

To assess the ability of sucrose or a pacifier to *prevent* an increase in either crying, activity, or heart rate, the object that the infant was sucking—either a pacifier or his or her own hand—was removed from the mouth and replaced with a pacifier, sucrose, or both within 5 sec. As will be shown, sucrose neither reduced nor prevented these infants from experiencing profound behavioral disruption. Accordingly, calming tests were stopped within 1 min and prevention tests within 2 min of initiation, and the infants were given back their pacifiers. On those occasions when the infants' brought their hands to their mouths during the course of sucrose delivery, the experiment continued because the infants found it very disturbing to have their hands removed from their mouths. Although this resulted in uneven experimental protocols (the sessions differed in length as a result), it was highly informative.

RESULTS

The Effects of Sucrose Alone

Sucrose delivered intraorally did not calm methadone infants (whose mothers may also have used cocaine during pregnancy). Moreover, sucrose did not prevent them from becoming extraordinarily agitated when the pacifier was removed from their mouths. (These findings are presented graphically in Fig. 14.)

Figure 14*a* shows baseline crying, crying during sucrose administration, and postadministration crying in a representative methadone infant test. Although sucrose was taken avidly, crying started *immediately* after the syringe was removed (at 30 sec) at the baseline rate. In this particular experiment, the 18% solution, which was delivered at 30-sec intervals, simply did not affect crying behavior even though, in terms of both volume and concentration, the dose was greater than that which quieted normal infants very effectively. Crying did stop, however, once the baby put his hand in his mouth. One might argue that the infant's behavior had become so disrupted and disorganized that sucrose could not restore equilibrium. In fact, even when experimental sessions began with the infants in a state of behavioral equilibrium, achieved through allowing them to such a pacifier, extreme crying could not be prevented by sucrose administration when the pacifier was removed.

Figure 14*b* presents heart rate profiles obtained during the test. Sucrose did not reduce this infant's heart rate from its initial 210 BPM. In fact, heart rate accelerated until the infant firmly secured his hand in his mouth. We should note here that these infants could distinguish between the taste of sucrose and that of water. That they could was unmistakable, the video-

FIG. 14.—The effects of sucrose administration (0.5 ml of 18% sucrose solution delivered at the times indicated by the arrows) on crying (Fig. 14*a*), heart rate (Fig. 14*b*), and activity (scale in text) (Fig. 14*c*) of a representative infant born to a woman who was maintained on methadone during pregnancy. Crying and hand-to-mouth behavior are shown in terms of duration (percentage), and heart rate in terms of beats per minute, for a given 30-sec interval. For ease of comparison, hand-mouth behavior is presented in Fig. 14*d*, represented by filled histograms. Note the elevated heart rate levels relative to normal infants even after stability has been attained.

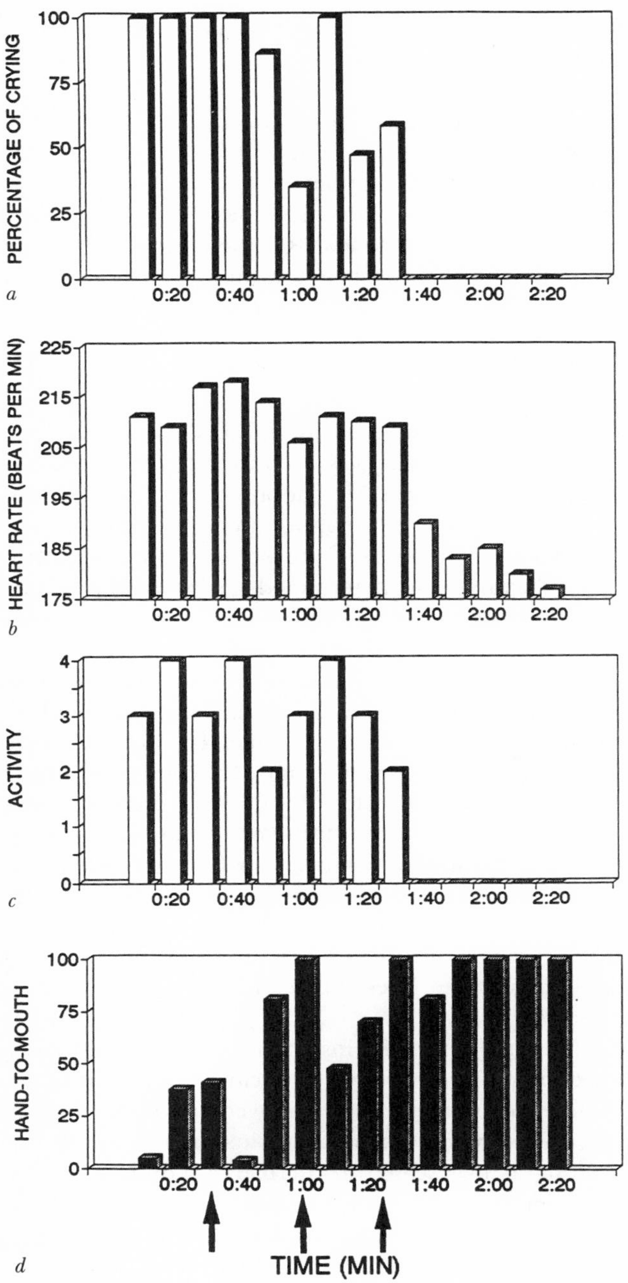
PERCENTAGE OF CRYING
100
75
50
25
0
0:20
0:40
1:00
1:20
1:40
2:00
2:20
a
HEART RATE (BEATS PER MIN)
225
215
205
195
185
175
b
ACTIVITY
4
3
2
1
0
c
HAND-TO-MOUTH
100
75
50
25
0
d
TIME (MIN)

tapes of the infants' behavior revealing that sucrose was always taken avidly and savored, water only rarely so.

Figure 14*c* demonstrates that sucrose did not affect activity levels. Activity was determined by whether the infant had his hand in his mouth. He moved vigorously about, seemingly in search of his hand. As with crying, the ineffectiveness of sucrose cannot be understood from the perspective of initial infant state because calm methadone infants became hyperactive in a matter of seconds only seconds after the pacifier was removed prior to sucrose treatment. The contrast between these infants and calm or agitated control infants is stark, especially considering that the methadone infants were on phenobarbital and occasionally paregoric and received 0.5 ml of 18% sucrose every 30 sec as opposed to 0.1 ml of 12% sucrose every 60 sec, as did the normal population.

The abrupt change in the behavior of the methadone infant that started at 1 min, 30 sec, can be understood entirely from the infant's success in keeping his hand in his mouth. Methadone infants managed to achieve this at every opportunity. It was common for an infant to trap an arm by rolling on its side and then reach for the captured hand with its mouth. The clarity as well as the repetitive and determined nature of this act were striking. Once the hand was seated in the mouth, it could not be readily dislodged.

This pattern differs from that shown by normal infants, for whom hand-mouth behavior was a consequence of sucrose administration after calm had been established. In methadone infants, hand-mouth activity was *the* determinant of calmness and state change. It is possible that these infants were perpetually hungry (see below) and that sucrose was not sufficient to assuage their need or motive state. This does not account, however, for the fact that sucrose had no apparent influence on any of the other measures. Our experience with normal infants who had not eaten (suckled) for 6 hours has been that the effects that sucrose had on them were similar to but less powerful than those that it had on less deprived normal infants. Thus, sucrose calming did in fact occur in normal infants, whereas for methadone infants—even ones that had been recently fed—sucrose was simply ineffective.

Figure 15 demonstrates the instantaneous and profound quieting that occurs when crying infants were given pacifiers and the instantaneous onset of crying when the pacifiers were removed: an unflavored pacifier stops crying, prevents its increase, and maintains calm in awake methadone infants for as long as it is seated in the baby's mouth. Crying begins again immediately when the pacifier is removed. This held whether the pacifier was dipped in water or sucrose. For methadone infants, sucrose has no protracted effect once the sucrose-coated pacifier is removed.

The same pattern held for activity. As shown in Figure 16, once methadone infants were given a pacifier, activity immediately dropped to and

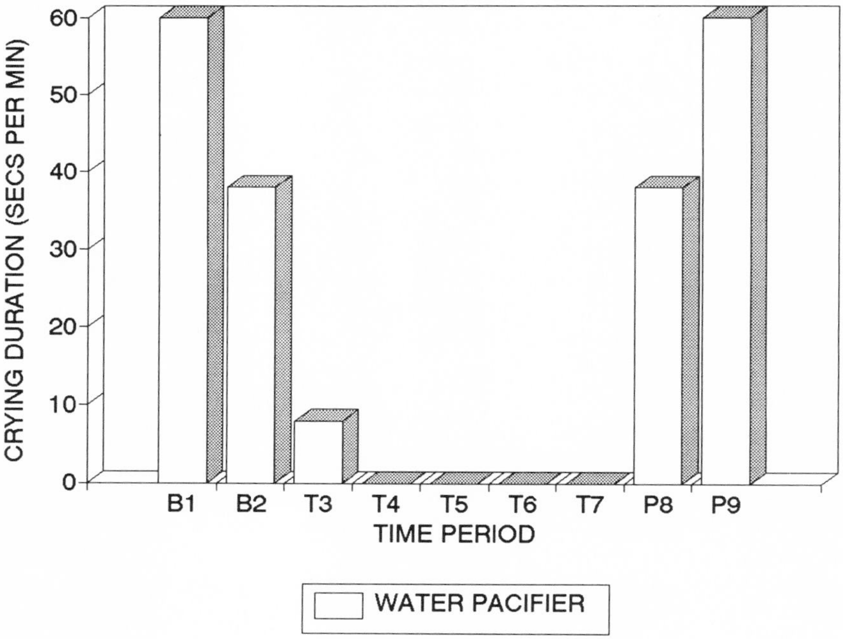

FIG. 15.—The effects of the administration of a water-coated pacifier on methadone infants ($N = 4$), shown in terms of the reduction or cessation of crying on administration and the resumption of crying on removal of the pacifier.

stayed at naught. Again, very high levels of activity recurred almost immediately after the pacifier was removed. The presence of a pacifier, therefore, had very similar effects on both crying and activity in methadone and normal infants. Levels drop to zero immediately, and this reduced level of energy expenditure is sustained for the duration of pacifier stimulation. When the pacifier is removed, infants again start to cry and become active.

As would be predicted from the crying and activity profiles, methadone infants' heart rate was extraordinarily high during periods when they were not allowed to suck on a pacifier and dropped precipitously and remained at stable levels when they were (albeit at levels that were much higher—ca. 165–175 BPM—than the normal infant resting baseline, as expected because of the lack of endogenous opioids). Heart rate immediately started to increase linearly when the pacifier was removed. We returned the pacifier when heart rate reached 215 BPM. Thus, within the context of the present study, methadone infants (at least those on phenobarbital) can be soothed and quieted and their attention engaged by a pacifier but not by sucrose taste.

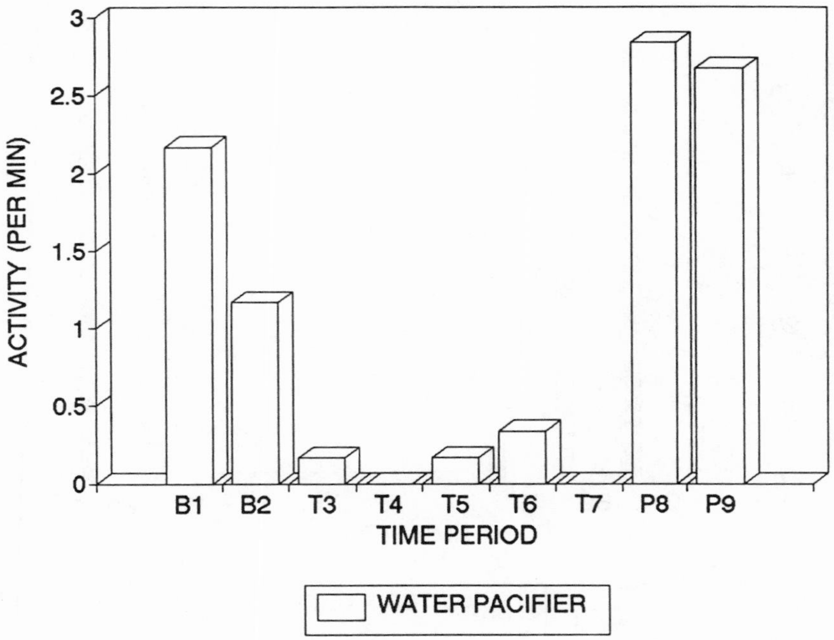

FIG. 16.—Reduction of gross motor activity achieved through the administration of a water-coated pacifier to the four methadone infants. Effects shown are before (B1–B2), during (T3–T7), and after (P8–P9) treatment.

Effects of Pacifier and Sucrose Administration

One could argue that taste alone was not effective because it could not engage the central system but that, once the infant was calmed by the pacifier, taste effects would be revealed, as they were earlier in normal agitated infants for whom pacifier-sucrose stimulation caused a decrease in heart rate that was sustained after the pacifier was removed. If this interpretation is true, it implies that the methadone infants' deficit can be understood on attentional grounds and not as reflecting an inaccessibility of motivational systems to taste stimulation. Administering sucrose-coated pacifiers to methadone infants did not cause a protracted calm or bradycardia after the pacifier was removed. Thus, sucrose was ineffective even when the infant had been calmed. In conjunction with the inability of sucrose to prevent crying and the attendant hyperactivity and elevated heart rate, we tentatively conclude that, for newborn humans who had experienced prolonged in utero exposure to methadone, endogenous opioids cannot be released by the taste of sucrose.

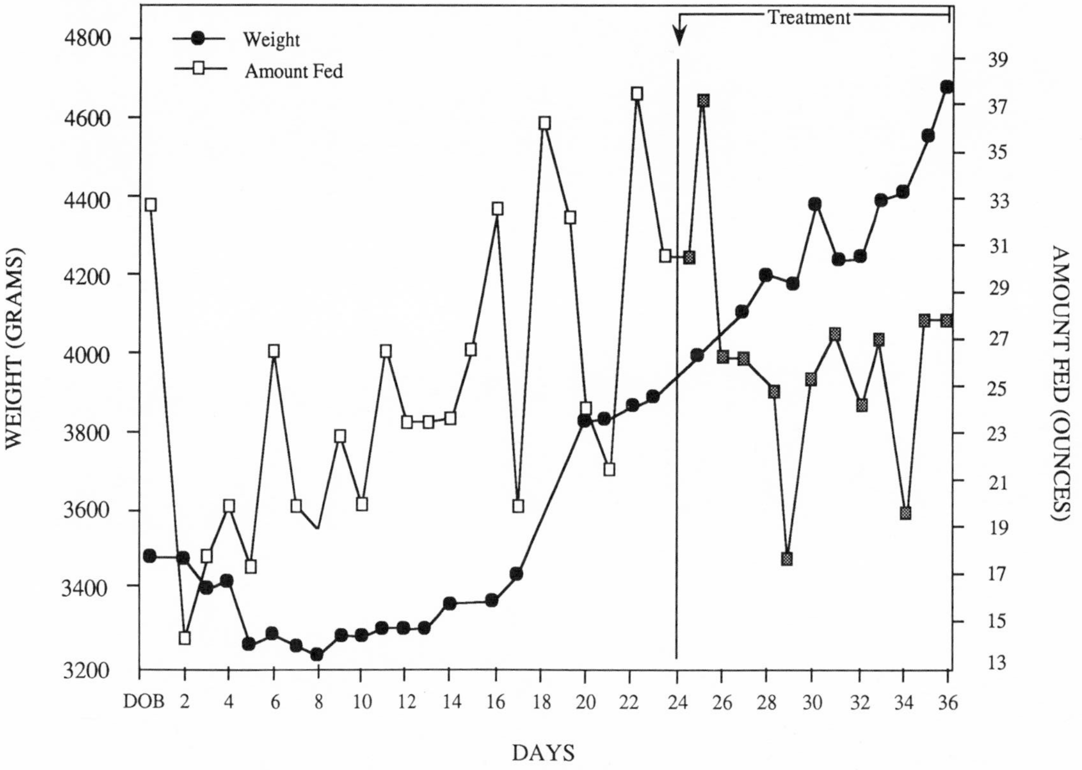

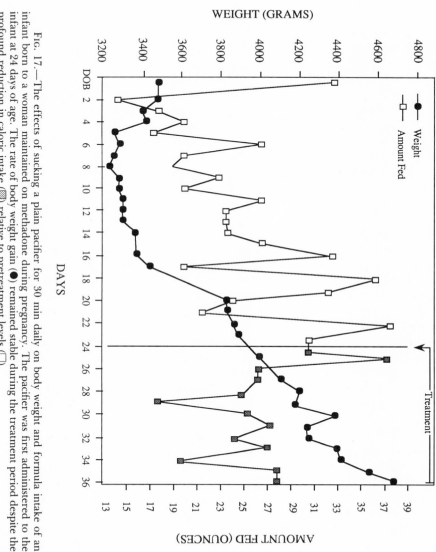

FIG. 17.—The effects of sucking a plain pacifier for 30 min daily on body weight and formula intake of an infant born to a woman maintained on methadone during pregnancy. The pacifier was first administered to the infant at 24 days of age. The rate of body weight gain (●) remained stable during the treatment period despite the profound reduction in caloric intake (▩) relative to pretreatment levels (□).

Case Report: Pacification, Feeding, and Growth in an Infant Born to a Methadone-Maintained Woman

Methadone infants can grow at normal rates, but they require supplemental feedings if they are to do so. This itself poses a problem because of the additional work demanded of the digestive system, which in these infants is already under considerable stress from hypermotility due to the functional absence of endogenous opioids. Accordingly, in order to ease these infants' digestive burden, we evaluated the hypothesis that increased intake was caused by the increased long-term energy expenditure that accompanied crying. It followed that, if crying could be reduced and energy utilization enhanced (Woodson, Drinkwin, & Hamilton, 1985) by sucking a pacifier, then, correspondingly, intake would be reduced with no cost to body weight gain. This was undertaken for 12 days in a single infant born to a methadone-maintained woman. For 30 consecutive min daily, an experimenter ensured that the pacifier was firmly seated in the infant's mouth. When possible, this care was extended by nursing staff.

As shown in Figure 17, this regimen was successful during our 12-day effort. The infant maintained his growth trajectory while receiving fewer daily feedings and total calories. Obviously, this experiment demands replication with an eye toward maximizing the amount of time the infant spends sucking on a pacifier throughout the day-night cycle, a difficult proposition for nursing staffs that are chronically overworked. The increased efforts might be worthwhile if they lead to more rapid recovery from exposure to methadone or heroin, less behavioral stress on the infant, and increased relief of cardiovascular and gastrointestinal stress. It is of considerable interest that nonnutritive sucking reduces heart rate in normal infants (Woodson et al., 1985). Moreover, nonnutritive sucking also allows premature infants to gain weight more rapidly than pair-fed controls (Bernbaum, Pereira, Watkins, & Peckham, 1983; Field et al., 1982). The short-term investment of additional effort is reminiscent of Schanberg and Field's (1987; Field et al., 1986) demonstration that stroking premature infants, especially on the back of the neck, leads to more rapid weight gain and earlier hospital discharge. These profound changes, which are now reported in three populations of infants, deserve further exploration. Finally, in conjunction with those obtained from rat studies, the present findings support the idea that, in human infants, the effectiveness of sucrose is mediated by neural systems in which some of the critical elements are opioid. Implications of gustatory quiescence for normal ontogeny will be developed below.

V. DISCUSSION: THE PSYCHOBIOLOGY OF EARLY MOTHER-INFANT INTERACTIONS

Here we discuss four interdependent issues concerning the psychobiology of early mother-infant relationships: energetics, changes in the infant's brain caused by stimulation by the mother, the development of early motivation systems, and specific long-term consequences of early state changes. First, we provide a brief summary of the major findings:

1. Microliter volumes of sucrose (100 μl of sucrose has a volume about the same as 1 drop of water) cause profound and relatively enduring state changes in agitated 1–3-day-old full-term, normal human infants. Sucrose taste reduces crying and gross motor activity but increases the incidence of hand-mouth integration. Some effects are striking, as when the occasional infant manages to get both hands in his or her mouth. Others are subtle, as when an infant might open only one eye for a while, look about, and then shut it. Sucrose taste influences cardiovascular function as well. During the 5-min period of sucrose administration, heart rate falls by about 20% in agitated infants and by about 7%–8% in calm infants.

2. The effectiveness of sucrose depends on context. Sucrose did not cause eye opening in either calm or agitated infants. Sucrose does not further calm infants exhibiting already low rates of spontaneous activity (although "basement" effects must be considered), nor did it cause them to bring their hands to their mouths or to open their eyes. Water caused three of the eight calm infants to cry.[5]

[5] Calm infants who were given water to drink often rejected it, and three cried on receiving it. This has been our experience in other studies as well, involving infants up to 4 weeks of age. This may be understood from the perspective of water balance and renal (kidney) hemodynamics. The newborn's kidneys are immature and specialize in water conservation. This works well for milk, which is of the same tonicity as the infant's body fluids. It is problematic, however, for nondehydrated infants who are drinking water. In the short term (i.e., within minutes), water will be retained and dilute the body fluids. A 1.5% decrease in concentration in adults disrupts motor coordination. Frank water intoxication occurs with 4.5% dilution. The margin for error is small. Dehydrated adult

3. Oral stimulation via a pacifier achieves the same effects as does sucrose, but with three noteworthy differences. First, there is generally a flurry of activity and excitement for 3–5 sec when the pacifier is initially placed in the mouth—this, of course, is common in normal circumstances of nursing. Second, once the pacifier is seated, changes are induced instantaneously. Third, the calming effects of pacification are fleeting: reduced crying and cardiovascular output and increased hand-mouth contact are reversed within 30 sec of the removal of the water-coated pacifier and rapidly approach baseline levels. If the pacifier has been sucrose-flavored, however, pacifier effects endure.

4. Different central mechanisms mediate pacifier and sucrose effects. While sucrose taste did not reduce crying, heart rate, and activity levels of infants born to methadone-maintained mothers, the pacifier did, quite effectively. This demonstrates the specificity of the deficit in methadone infants and fosters an appreciation of the behavioral and physiological ramifications arising from the lack of central endogenous opioids.

These findings can best be understood from the perspectives of the behavioral and physiological consequences of mother-infant contact and milk exchange, mechanisms that underlie these changes, motive states mobilized by these changes, and learning opportunities presented to the infant by altered motivation. These four issues take on particular meaning when one considers what the infant's and mother's complementary tasks are. From our perspective, infants have two "jobs." The first is to grow and develop maximally in good health. The second is to learn accurately about the "postnest" environment at the least risk possible while still in the nest. This is especially important for omnivorous animals such as rats and humans who must know about food safety, among other things.

PHYSIOLOGICAL CONSEQUENCES OF MOTHER-INFANT CONTACT AND OF MILK EXCHANGE

The current discussion focuses on early mother-infant interactions in mammals through the lens of biology. Rather than necessarily viewing infants as incomplete adults who have not attained mature levels of anatomi-

---

rats drinking water prevent water intoxication by terminating drinking at the first signs of overhydration (Blass & Hall, 1976; Hall & Blass, 1975); they eat food, thereby returning the concentration to normal, and excrete the excess water in a highly dilute urine. At the time of drinking cessation caused by dilution, rats often make aversive gestures such as scraping their muzzle on the floor. To prevent overhydration, human infants can only avoid water. They cannot rely on obtaining food or, owing to immature renal capacity, excreting excess water. In the future, researchers using water as a control substance should take into account the possibility that it might be aversive.

cal, physiological, and behavioral differentiation, it may prove useful to conceptualize infants as having their own highly specialized adaptations that differ qualitatively from those of adults. This is clearly seen in ingestive behavior. The gastrointestinal tract of infant mammals is specialized to process milk. Dentition is delayed. Negative pressure and manipulation by tongue and soft palate maximize milk extraction from nipple and breast. The facial musculature, in conjunction with an abundant flow of saliva, establishes a vacuum seal on nipple or breast (Epstein, Blass, Batshaw, & Parks, 1970). Newborns come prepared with specialized rooting and probing reflexes that establish and maintain contact with breast or nipple. Both digestive and behavioral specializations disappear by weaning.

Strategies for optimizing energy gain and reducing energy loss during early development are seen regularly in behavior and physiology and are often dramatic. Rats lack direct control over milk intake through suckling until they start to eat food directly from the environment at the onset of weaning. In an experimental setting, 10-day-old rats withdrew milk from a series of lactating dams by suckling until their stomachs became so full that milk refluxed up the esophagus and out the nares. This reflux occurred after the infants had spontaneously taken about 22% of their body weight in milk (Cramer & Blass, 1983). Normally, of course, the mother limits the amount of milk available (Henning, 1981). But, from the infant's perspective, the volume of milk that it ingests when suckling is constrained, not by normal physiological signals, but by the tensile properties of the stomach and gastrointestinal tract, which could no longer expand to accommodate additional milk after the remarkable increase of almost one-quarter of the animal's body weight in a single meal. The magnitude of this phenomenon in which physiological control is suspended in deference to caloric intake highlights the importance of maximizing energy gain and minimizing energy loss.

Behavioral strategies that minimize energy loss are not limited to ingestive behavior. Infants also compensate behaviorally for their physical vulnerability and thermal lability. They seek and maintain contact, thereby reducing energy loss. In nested, furless rats that have minimal physiological thermoregulatory capacities (Spiers & Adair, 1986), normal body temperatures are actively defended by huddling (Alberts, 1978; Alberts & Brunjes, 1978; Cosnier, 1965), at a reduced metabolic cost (Stainer, 1975; Taylor, 1960). Isolated animals seek thermoneutrality (i.e., nest temperature) on a thermal gradient (Kleitman & Satinoff, 1982).

From the biological perspective, the rat mother is the infant's primary source of heat and its exclusive source of energy. She actively maintains an insulated, thermally stable nest area for her infants, thereby protecting them against heat loss (Kinder, 1927). Simple contact alone causes two immediate thermal changes in the infant. First, heat is obtained from the mother through conduction. Second, heat loss is reduced because the infant is now part of the larger unit and its surface-mass ratio is lowered dramatically (i.e., there is proportionately less surface area for heat transfer). The mother also provides milk (the composition of which varies according to infants' age) to sustain growth, and, as shown here, the act of sucking itself appears to cause energy conservation.

Human parenting, of course, also reflects sensitivity to infant heat loss by conduction. In Western industrial societies, human infants—newborns especially—are kept wrapped and in warm rooms (i.e., they are insulated against heat loss). In nonindustrial societies, infants are often housed in slings or cradle boards worn by the mother (Barr, Bakeman, Konner, & Adomson, 1991). This contact cuts down on energy loss and provides "contact comfort," reducing (eliminating) the costly act of crying. Behavioral, physiological, and anatomical specializations that are energy conserving and energy repleting have evolved together. Stated simply, every calorie lost in energy expenditure (whether in the process of thermoregulation, crying, or activity) is a calorie stolen from infant growth and development.

A second avenue of energy loss, well known to a weight-conscious public, is exercise. Oxygen consumption increases by 10% during brief (2-min) crying bouts (Rao, Blass, Brignol, Marino, & Glass, 1993). It is simply not known how energetically costly sustained crying is to the developing organism. It certainly is not trivial; recall the methadone infant who did not cry while sucking a pacifier, thereby reducing his energy expenditure and consequently his food intake by about 20%, and still maintained his weight gain trajectory. This may not have been due to reduced crying alone; savings through nonnutritive suckling have also been documented in normal infants (Woodson & Hamilton, 1986) and in premature infants (Bernbaum et al., 1983; Field et al., 1982; Measel & Anderson, 1979). How relatively brief periods of sucking enhance net energy gain is not known.

Crying is another strategy that ultimately reduces heat loss. Isolated, wet, or distressed infants cry. Crying is an effective means of obtaining adults' attention and care in all species studied, including humans (Barr et al., 1991). Although crying itself is energetically costly, its occurrence in animals, at least, is an expression of pain or perceived danger demanding the parents' immediate attention and the obvious benefits—one might consider crying to be an emergency response.

In considering the evolutionary history of crying, one is impressed with the limited sets of circumstances under which crying occurs among primates in the wild and among human infants who remain in close contact with their mothers throughout the first 4 years. Infant primates cry when they have been dropped while being carried or when they have sustained serious injury. Crying, therefore, has a high pain threshold. Crying is ecologically dangerous because primate cries are loud, piercing, and carry a considerable distance, thereby endangering infant, mother, and kin. Crying infants are attended to immediately by the closest adult, generally the mother or another female or, in their absence, the males. The energetics issue, plus the evolutionary considerations of the mothers' (adults') rapid response to a behavior exhibited only after a high threshold has been crossed, should make us reconsider what has become a standard guideline for human infant crying in the West, namely, that crying can normally (i.e., acceptably) occur for 2 hours daily (Brazelton, 1962). On what basis can this be supported?

In fact, crying can be markedly reduced in normal infants simply by increasing the amount of time that an infant is carried daily. According to Barr (1990), who has written thoughtfully on this issue, infants in Western cultures cry for longer durations than do infants raised in cultures, like those in our not too distant past, in which the crying infant is attended to with alacrity by adults. Barr has demonstrated that increased *noncontingent* carrying markedly reduced daily crying by shortening bout length but not bout frequency. Increased holding may have reduced affective tone while leaving the infants responsive to events, such as hunger or discomfort, that elicit crying. Whether this reduction in tone, tension, and energy expenditure casts a long-lasting influence on human infant development is open to empirical assessment. That crying can be decreased by means of brief periods of supplementary carrying is reminiscent of the protracted effects of modest amounts of supplementary sucking on growth described above in premature infants. It would be interesting to know whether the infants whom Barr studied gained more weight during the experimental period.

MECHANISMS UNDERLYING CHANGE

Opioid Integration

Our recognition of infants' physical vulnerability and their needs for adequate contact, warmth, and nutrition to reduce energy expenditure and promote growth frames our view of how, through the context of mother-infant interaction, endogenous opioids contribute to the processes of growth and differentiation. All the changes reported here that were induced by sucrose taste, and presumably mediated by the release of endogenous opioids, share the common functions of energy conservation and replenishment. Crying stops, as does hyperactivity. Heart rate drops by about 20%, oxygen consumption by 10%. To the extent that bringing the hands to the mouth may be part of a primitive feeding system, the taste of sucrose, presumably through central opioid mediation, engages a feeding system or enhances the salience of hunger signals in agitated newborns.[6] The present findings and those from animal studies start to reveal how mother's milk may influence newborn mammals. Three pathways have been identified: gustatory, postingestive, and postabsorptive.

Gustatory.—The present report points to gustatory mediation of sucrose calming as opposed to a postingestive mode. First, changes started during the first 1–2 minutes of delivery. Second, the volumes delivered were vanishingly small. In fact, Barr et al. (1991) quieted human infants with a single 250-μl delivery of sucrose. In newborn rats, Blass et al. (1991) have achieved pain reduction within 20 sec of the injection of 20 μl of milk into the mouth. That the volumes involved are so small and the time periods so brief mitigates against postabsorptive effects, and, because the fluid delivery constituted the human infants' first experience with sucrose (and the infant rats' first experience with milk), taste could not have induced conditioned postingestive response patterns. The pacifier's route of action is, of course, entirely gustatory.

Postingestive.—The preceding notwithstanding, it seems very likely that, through its fat component, milk also acts postingestionally when normal volumes are absorbed. In particular, the gut hormone cholecystokinin (CCK), which is normally released by fat perfusing the intestines (Lewis & Williams, 1990), is a potent quieting agent in rats when delivered into the peritoneal cavity in doses of 2–20 μg per kilogram of body weight (Weller & Blass, 1988). CCK's action is not opioid mediated because it is not compromised by naltrexone (Weller & Blass, 1988). Moreover CCK may be active under physiological circumstances: Blass and Shide (1993) have shown that devazepide—a specific CCK antagonist—prevents oral infusions of milk and fat from decreasing the number of vocalizations emitted by isolated 10-day-old rats; sucrose quieting is not affected by devazepide.

Postabsorptive.—The evidence for postabsorptive mechanisms is encouraging but not as yet compelling. The milk of a number of mammals, including humans, contains beta-casomorphine, a morphine-like substance that is released in the intestine from the casein fraction of milk (Brandl & Tesmacher, 1979). Beta-casomorphine injected systemically or directly into the brains of 10-day-old rats elevated heat-escape latencies, and this too was naloxone reversible (Blom & Blass, 1993). It is not known, however, whether beta-casomorphine is active behaviorally under normal circumstances. At physiological levels, it may not be able to survive degradation by the liver

[6] This last idea is supported by substantial pharmacological and behavioral literatures on opioid influences on ingestive behavior. Adult rats that receive morphine injections increase feeding—the increase is preferentially directed toward fats and sweets (Marks-Kaufman et al., 1985). This behavior pattern is also observed in mildly stressed rats and humans—in rats, the effects are blocked by naloxone administration (Antelman, Rowland, & Fisher, 1976).

and may not be able to penetrate the blood-brain barrier to gain access to the brain. These issues can be answered empirically.

Nonopioid Integration

Until now we have focused this discussion on the gustatory and ingestive consequences of milk and their mediation. We now address the question of how mothers calm and comfort their infants and reduce energy loss in ways that do not involve ingestion. Multiple pathways are at play here in the form of vestibular stimulation, contact, heat transfer, oral stimulation by breast or nipple, and the motor patterns of suckling and grasping that they elicit. The effects are at least as dramatic as those caused by oral infusions of sucrose or milk. Pathways for contact comfort are mediated by systems that do not appear to have opioid components. This assertion is based on two rat studies in which naloxone administration did not interfere with the mother's ability to quiet isolated infants through contact (Blass et al., 1990; Winslow & Insel, 1990) and on the current studies in human infants born to women who had been maintained on methadone throughout pregnancy. The pacifier calmed these latter infants, on whom substantial volumes of concentrated sucrose solution had no effect.

Contact calms, as we know personally and anecdotally. Experimental data support our subjective impressions. Gunnar, Fisch, and Malone (1984) reported a 30% decrease in crying during circumcision, brought about by allowing infants to suck a pacifier (this finding has been replicated by Blass & Hoffmeyer, 1991). Even subtle forms of contact can have remarkable and protracted effects. As indicated earlier, gently stroking the nape of the neck of premature infants markedly accelerated their growth rate and led to a significantly reduced hospital stay (Field et al., 1986; Schanberg & Field, 1987). Protracted (30 min or more) nonnutritive sucking facilitated growth (through either reduced energy expenditure or enhanced metabolic efficiency) in one methadone infant in the present study. Reduced energy loss through nonnutritive sucking and/or increased efficiency has also been reported in normal (Woodson & Hamilton, 1986, 1988) and premature (Bernbaum et al., 1983; Field et al., 1982; Measel & Anderson, 1979) human infants.

An issue that is fundamental to our understanding of how motivation processes develop concerns interactions among opioid- and nonopioid-mediated systems. The interactions are multidirectional, and at this point we know neither the pharmacological nor the behavioral rules of combination. Sometimes the combination is additive, as when a pacifier and sucrose are more effective than a pacifier alone in reducing crying during circumcision (Blass & Hoffmeyer, 1991). It may also be multiplicative. Thus, Blass et al.

(1993) have recently found that morphine simply added to the antinociceptive effects of contact but multiplied those of suckling in terms of both magnitude and duration of effect. Sometimes combining treatments actually detracts from their potency—a number of animal studies make this point strongly.[7]

The unavailability of one system may enhance the function of the other. Thus, exaggerated calming was induced in methadone infants by the presence of a pacifier or by the infants themselves bringing their hands to their mouths. For the normal infants in our study, sucking a pacifier shadowed taste-induced changes. This was seen most clearly in the lack of additivity in hand-mouth behavior, heart rate decline, and eye opening, all of which were at levels caused by the presence of a pacifier alone. Yet taste did contribute because crying cessation, hand-mouth coordination, and low heart rate continued after the sweetened pacifier was removed, whereas the removal of a water-pacifier induced crying, elevated heart rate, and reduced hand-mouth behavior (see also Smith et al., 1990). Identifying and understanding the rules of combination are central to any analysis of emotional development because, each time the infant is nursed by the mother, various opioid and nonopioid mechanisms underlying state changes are naturally engaged.

Finally, contact appears to be every bit as potent a reinforcer as taste, possibly more so. Alberts and May (1984) have demonstrated that the opportunity for preweanling rats to huddle with a nonlactating female was as reinforcing as suckling with milk letdown. In fact, a warm tube served as well. Thus, newborn mammals have available to them at least two calming and reinforcing systems that have different temporal behavioral characteristics. They are mediated, in part, by separate neurotransmitters. The two processes have access to the same energy-conserving effector systems, to the same emotional systems that calm and reduce heart rate (Sananes, Gaddy, & Campbell, 1988), and to the motivational systems that maintain contact with caregivers.

Figure 18 provides a model of how nursing-suckling interactions may cause the energy-conserving changes that we have described. It builds on the model presented in Figure 12 above and serves to provide direction for future research. In this model, stress or pain gives rise to crying, to which the mother responds by nursing (although nursing, of course, also occurs in the absence of crying). Contact itself, especially suckling, markedly affects

[7] Bodnar's studies (e.g., Kiefel, Paul, & Bodnar, 1989) of nonopioid-opioid antagonism are especially interesting. He has demonstrated a *diminution* in morphine-induced (opioid) analgesia in rats that had just experienced the stress of a cold water swim. The latter treatment alone causes a nonopioid-mediated analgesia. The antagonism cannot be understood on the basis of incapacitation because subtractivity occurs even at low doses. The causes of subtractivity and its functional significance have remained elusive.

all the measures that we have employed, apparently through systems that do not have an opioid component and that can be designated as on-off. Milk affects behavior in at least three ways, two of which are opioid mediated. The nonopioid means is through the release of CCK, which may sensitize contact or suckling systems or may itself act directly on the integrator. It is interesting in this regard that CCK actions are not graded but are also on-off (Weller & Blass, 1988).

Milk influences behavior via opioid pathways activated by the taste of milk. There may also be a direct opioid contribution through the central action of beta-casomorphine. The onset of opioid effects relative to those of the pacifier is slower, and there is also a relatively long time of offset. Although the *time courses* of onset and offset are graded, the *magnitude* of crying reduction caused by sucrose is not. According to Blass and Smith (1992), once a threshold in sucrose concentration or volume had been crossed, suprathreshold volumes and concentrations all were equally effective in arresting crying and protracting the quiet period. Blass and Shide (1993) have also obtained the same results in rats. We suggest that the system that *transduces* taste afferents to calming efferents is on-off because both the afferent and the efferent limbs of the system act in a graded manner. Human infants discriminate among sucrose concentrations, as shown by changes in sucking rate (Lipsitt et al., 1976) and volume intake (Desor et al., 1973). Moreover, heat withdrawal latencies of newborn rats were linearly affected by morphine dose (Blass et al., 1991). Accordingly, although the onset and offset times of sucrose influences are graded, the magnitude of effect is not, at least for crying.

MOTIVATION CONSIDERATIONS

When activated alone, either nonopioid or opioid components of the mother-infant care system are rewarding. Specifically, rats seek contact with anesthetized dams (Kenny & Blass, 1977) and among themselves (Alberts & Brunjes, 1978) and prefer an odor that had predicted and had been associated with CCK injections (Weller & Blass, 1990; Weller, Blass, Smith, & Gibbs, 1993). Likewise, rats prefer an odor associated with fat or sucrose infusions (Shide & Blass, 1991). Preference for odors associated with oral sucrose or fat can be blocked at the time of acquisition by naloxone. Preference expression can also be stopped by naloxone at the time of testing. We next explore these motivation issues.

Because diverse forms of stimulation provided by rat and human mothers can cause different short- and long-term changes in infant behavior and physiology, an evaluation of which motivational systems are available to newborns, of how they may be open to external influences, and of their

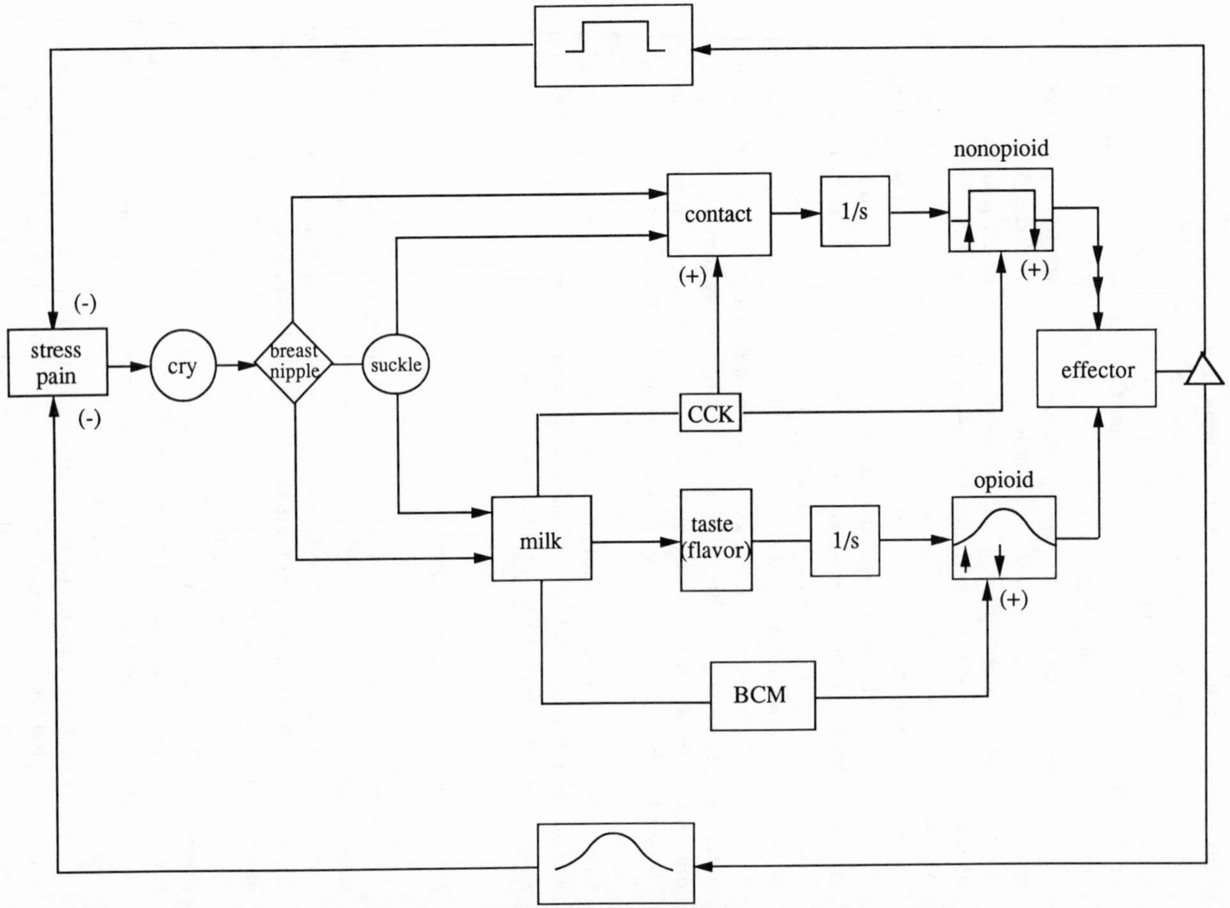

stress
pain
(-)
(-)
cry
breast
nipple
suckle
contact
(+)
1/s
nonopioid
(+)
effector
CCK
milk
taste
(flavor)
1/s
opioid
(+)
BCM

capacity to cause enduring change is called for. From the perspectives of evolutionary biology and developmental psychology, both contact and gustatory stimulation are ideal vehicles through which infants can learn about their mother. Two conservative systems are at work here.[8] First, contact and sucrose both reduce energy loss, as documented by Rao et al. (1993) and implied here, and milk, of course, provides the calories, water, nutrients, and antibodies necessary to sustain action and growth. Second, both forms of stimulation elicit complex motor patterns of approaching, rooting into the mother, and suckling that ensure protracted contact with the mother and facilitate milk letdown (for a review, see Brake, Shair, & Hofer, 1988). Thus, infants receive commodities from their mother that are vital for growth and to which they are attracted. Moreover, the infants themselves are active players in obtaining these substances. Thus, whether one favors the primacy of sensory (Pfaffmann, 1964) or motor (Glickman & Schiff, 1967; Lorenz, 1943) stimulation in the genesis of reward or changes in central state (Bechara, Harrington, Nader, & van der Kooy, 1992; Wise & Bozarth, 1984) or that of central-peripheral interactions (Valenstein, Cox, & Kakolewski, 1968) or contingent changes based on what is available periodically in the environment (Premack, 1962), the nursing-suckling setting makes available to the infant all these possibilities for long-term change in behavior vis-à-vis the individual who is providing that care.

From the evolutionary perspective, recognition and bonding between parents and infants are advantageous to infants in both the short term (for

[8] As it is used here, "conservative" refers to the traits in question being conserved in all mammals.

FIG. 18.—Model incorporating oral, postingestive, and postabsorptive effects of suckling on infant state and the mechanisms underlying those changes. The model builds on that presented in Fig. 12 above. The breast (nipple) in conjunction with suckling provides tactile (and pressure) stimulation and milk to the infant. Contact is transduced (1/s) via nonopioid mechanisms to the central mediator of each physiological and behavioral effector system evaluated in these experiments. Upward and downward arrows in each box represent stimulus onset and offset, respectively. According to this model, milk is thought to affect infant state in three ways: through its taste (flavor); through mediation by opioid transduction (as described in Fig. 12 above); and through CCK, which uses a nonopioid system either to sensitize peripheral contact receptors or to affect the central integration of these signals directly. Milk also provides the infant with beta-casomorphine (BCM), which can influence central opioid receptors (although it is not known whether beta-casomorphine actually reaches the central receptors under normal circumstances). The respective effectors are activated by the central mediating processes. The nonopioid system is emphasized because during suckling per se it seems to be dominant. The integrator pattern is presented in series with the effector system to indicate the timing relations between stimulus onset and offset and the effector systems. It does not reflect the characteristics of effector integration. As in Fig. 12 above, the system is negative feedback in nature with no controlled variable because newborns, except when limited by sleep, will suckle when possible.

protection and maintenance) and the long (for education about relationships, food, and environmental safety). Contact with the mother and nursing provide opportunities for infants to learn about their mothers and express their motivation to remain close to them. It is not possible to say whether these considerations led to the morphological and behavioral changes that gave rise to nursing and suckling. They would appear to contribute to current behavioral patterns that could enhance an individual's fitness.

Can the infant use this information from the perspectives of learning and motivation? Newborns come prepared with many components of motive systems, but the systems do not seem to be completely formed. For example, motor patterns for a variety of behaviors are available, such as chewing, swallowing, drinking, and, in rats, lordosis (the downward curvature of the spine and the elevation of the rump normally shown by sexually receptive adult female rats). Infants seem to appreciate the consequences of certain actions; thus, rats press a lever contingently to receive infusions of milk into the mouth (Johanson & Hall, 1979) or electrical stimulation to the base of the brain (Moran et al., 1981) and discriminate between sides in a Y-maze that provide suckling opportunities as opposed to contact alone (Kenny & Blass, 1977). When the contingencies for receiving milk or electrical stimulation are reversed, even 3-day-old rats leave the paddle that had previously delivered milk or electrical current and push the second, previously unrewarding, paddle. The same holds for 9-day-old rats that traverse a Y-maze for contact alone or for suckling. These rats prefer the arm that allows nonnutritive suckling. When the location of suckling opportunity is reversed in the maze, rats quickly track the reversal, indicating some spatial representation capacities.

Human newborns can also effect changes in the world immediately surrounding them. By altering their rate of suckling according to schedule, they hasten the delivery of sugar solutions (Lipsitt, 1977) and the rate of presentation of a tape that produces the sound of their mother's voice reading familiar material (DeCasper & Fifer, 1980). Human infants can orient to odors previously paired with nursing or touch (Sullivan et al., 1991). Three-day-old humans prefer (i.e., look more often at) their mother's face over that of a stranger with similar facial features (Bushnell et al., 1983). Thus, altricial mammals (rats and humans, at least) are capable of goal-directed behavior around the time of birth and are sensitive to the consequences of their actions and to changes in environmental contingencies, and infant rats (Cramer, Pfister, & Haig, 1988) seem to have a representation of space and of themselves within that space. Infants will work for a variety of stimuli, ranging from brain reward to suckling, feeding, changes in temperature, or the sound of their mother's voice.

The question remains, however, whether this is a unitary system of affect or whether there are different systems that are bounded? If, as in adults, the systems are discrete, bounded, and modular, then engaging one motivational system—feeding, for example—should not, in principle, affect other motivational systems. Moreover, the memories of stimuli that predict or are associated with changes in one system should not influence other domains of motivation. Alternatively, if infants' motivational systems are not bounded, then stimulation, prediction, and associations that occur during one behavior in early development should influence the expression of other classes of behavior, including ones that may be available neurally but are not functional during infancy. This predicts that early intense experiences that occur within one context during development—suckling, for example—should influence later behaviors that do not share particular feature attributes but that do share general features such as increased arousal as in sexual behavior.

The resolution of these alternatives hinges on a number of factors. In our view, motivational systems are poorly specified early in development and may be restricted to the broad categories of excitation or calm. First, there do not appear to be boundaries among motor patterns of behavior, suckling being an important exception. Thus, stimulation—whether electrical, gustatory, or anogenital (licking by the mother)—that elicits one motor pattern in rats is likely to elicit *all* the patterns that are available to the animal (Hall, 1979; Moran, Schwartz, & Blass, 1983). Second, as seen here, stimulation that has never been experienced (sucrose, in this case) stops infant crying, the origin of which lies in a factor or factors not related to sucrose need or food privation. As we now show, these distinctions are of both theoretical and applied interest. Each will be discussed in turn.

Lack of Boundaries in Response Patterns during Excitation

Three experimental sources address this issue. First are the seminal studies of W. G. Hall on the ontogeny of ingestive behavior, second the studies of Moran and his colleagues on the effects of brain stimulation in infant rats, and third personal observations (of both EMB and others in the field) on the effects of the rat mother's stimulation of her infants through anogenital licking. We acknowledge at the outset that the first two forms of stimulation are unnatural. They are, however, revealing.

In Hall's studies, infant rats 1–15 days of age were deprived of contact with their mother and of her milk for up to 24 hours and were tested in a very warm ambience (33°C). They received commercial milk, through a thin tube surgically placed in the mouth. Under these circumstances, milk delivery in 1–6-day-old rats caused an explosion of behaviors that were not necessarily related to feeding, including gaping, rolling, licking, chewing, stretch responses (normally elicited by milk letdown from the nipple), and lordosis. By 9 days of age, the systems were sufficiently differentiated that only feeding behaviors were elicited; in fact, rats could eat from a focal location on the cage floor.

Moran and his colleagues (Moran et al., 1981; Moran et al., 1983) obtained parallel findings with brain stimulation in rats separated from their mothers for only a few hours and also tested in warm temperatures. Passing current through electrodes secured in the medial forebrain bundle (MFB) caused rats to work for more stimulation (Hall found this for intraoral milk infusions too) and, despite the absence of oral stimulation, elicited exactly the same action patterns as did milk infusions. According to Moran et al., the likelihood of a behavior occurring in 3- and 6-day-old rats bore no relation to the behavior that either preceded or followed it. Moreover, in 3- and 6-day-old rats that simultaneously received brain stimulation and milk infusions, the probability of *all* behaviors occurring increased markedly. By 9 days of age, however, milk infusions in rats receiving brain stimulation increased the probability of only feeding behavior and reduced the occurrence of behaviors (e.g., lordosis) that were not food related. In the absence of milk, the stretch response was almost always preceded by mouthing and the lordosis response almost never. Three-day-old rats had an equal likelihood of mouthing preceding stretch or lordosis behaviors during MFB stimulation. Stated differently, at first there seems to be a central excitatory state caused by milk infusions or by central brain stimulation that is available to all behaviors. By 9 days of age, this state is brought under the control of internal organization and of external events just as in adults, in whom stimulation-bound behaviors are elicited and directed by the affordances of the environment and are intrinsically organized (Valenstein et al., 1968).

Although to our knowledge there has been no formal documentation of the behaviors elicited by rat mothers when they stimulate the anogenital region of their infants, all the behaviors described by Hall and Moran are readily apparent and can be induced experimentally by gently stroking the rat's anogenital region with a soft artist's brush or a Q-tip. Thus, rat mothers regularly excite their pups when they void the infant's bladder while holding the infant close to their ventrum, which bears the odors that elicit suckling. This form of anogenital stimulation is rewarding to infant rats because they prefer the odors associated with such stimulation (Sullivan, Brake, Hofer, & Williams, 1986). Together, these data suggest, first, that motor patterns are interchangeable and, second, that the brain substrate involved in reward also gains control over all available motor patterns. We find it of considerable interest that this preference for odors associated with anogenital stimulation is mediated by central catecholamines because the major neurochemical systems in the MFB that support brain stimulation are also catecholaminergic (Moran, Sanburg, Antuoro, & Coyle, 1986).

The present studies provide additional evidence concerning nondifferentiated motivation systems during early infancy. Agitated, spontaneously crying human newborns made major physiological and behavioral energy-conserving adjustments to microliter intraoral deliveries of sucrose and to the tactile properties of a pacifier. Sucrose, fats, and milk apparently have access to opioid systems that cast far-reaching effects to bring the infants into a state of calm and energy conservation. The tactile route to these effectors is nonopioid. It seems to us, therefore, that two distinctive reward states exist in newborns and that each gains control over all the available motor patterns supported by that state: a short-lived excitatory state (probably catecholaminergic), normally elicited by vigorous external stimulation in which all behaviors become accessible for expression, and a calming system, engaged by taste (presumably opioid mediated) and touch (presumably nonopioid mediated), that reduces all manifestations of agitated behavior. To the extent that sweet taste and tactile stimulation essentially eliminate crying in normal isolated infants and markedly reduce crying caused by painful stimulation, we speculate that these effects too are global. It is of interest that, once infants have been calmed by the presence of a pacifier, they open their eyes, thereby learning about the visual characteristics of the agent of change.

We do not see the simultaneous existence of two reward states—an excitatory, energy-expending system and a calming, energy-conserving system—as inherently conflicting. Objectively, the two systems have very different operating characteristics, and we may hypothesize different functions for each system. Perspective on this may be gained from a consideration of the infant's sleep-wake cycle. Newborns spend the vast majority of the time asleep. There are, however, brief periods of extraordinary activity that surround parent-infant reunions. These reunions are highly arousing and objectively rewarding to infants and seem to have two functions. One allows the sucking system to be more readily engaged. The second—and this is conjecture—is that it supports normal brain development through catecholamine release. Newborn rats delivered by gentle cesarean section will die within 5–7 min if not stroked anogenitally by the experimenter (Pedersen & Blass, 1982). Learning is prevented in a number of systems during development by administering catecholamine blocking agents (Leon, 1992). These conjectures are potentially important because they are readily open to behavioral and anatomical verification.

The energy-conserving mechanism is of obvious import for normal development. Energy-conserving (Alberts, 1978) and highly specialized milk-seeking behavioral responses at the nipple are the two behavioral systems most advanced at birth in mammals. The changes described in this *Monograph,* which are mediated by gustatory-opioid factors and by orotactile nonopioid mechanisms, contribute broadly to energy conservation. Taken together, these three lines of evidence suggest complex and changing motivational systems in newborn and very young mammals. On the one hand, these systems share adult characteristics because infants' behavior can be directed and because infants can readily adjust to spatial and contingent changes in the environment. On the other hand, these systems differ in important ways from adult systems. Organized motor patterns are not bounded; rather, they flow one into the other. Early discriminations among states are commensurately broad; thus, affective state appears to represent a summation among inputs that do not have any obvious functional relation and that in adults are separable and independent. An implication of this point of view will be developed at the end of the next section.

Learning in Newborn Mammals

Infants are responsible for learning about the fluctuating aspects of the environment that they will encounter on leaving the natal setting. These include their own social status, the safety of foods from which they must select, safe geography, who their relatives are (in order to avoid both inbreeding and outbreeding; Bateson, 1978), and with whom to enter into alliances concerning the defense of territory and of young (Holmes, 1988). These tasks are not trivial; only 10% of the feral rat population attains reproductive age (Galef & Beck, 1990). Some die from disease. The reasons that the rest do not survive, however, are behavioral—they may not choose food wisely, may fall prey to predators, or may not find safe shelter.

In the mother, the infant has a teacher who has at least two characteristics. First, she has survived long enough to conceive, give birth, and nourish the infant and its siblings. Second, she is heavily invested (genetically) in the success of her infants. The mother, therefore, is the primary educator. She is responsible for selecting and maintaining a safe nest site. This location is especially important for her daughters, who, in general, do not disperse from the natal site. The mother educates all her young about food safety, first through her milk (Galef & Clark, 1971; Galef & Sherry, 1973), later by the example of eating safe foods in their presence (for a review of circumstances and mechanisms, see Galef & Beck, 1990). In primate societies, infants learn about their own social status through the actions of the mother. Thus, thanks to their mother's actions, the weanlings can leave the nest area with some knowledge of the outside world and some strategies for negotiating it.

The mother can educate because of the proximity that her infants maintain to her. According to Rosenblatt (1983), infants are born with a number of well-developed behavioral patterns that are elicited by specific features of the mother, such as warmth, touch, nipple texture, and nipple configuration. These patterns and their underlying affective states come under the control of other features that uniquely define an infant's particular mother and through which the infant is attracted to her. This line of reasoning is consonant with a substantial embryological literature indicating that motor pattern development precedes the advent of sensory selection (Oppenheim, 1982; Oppenheim & Haverkamp, 1986).

In the case of the organization of behavior after birth, Rosenblatt argues that the commonality of form among mammalian mothers in terms of warmth, fur, and lactation has also yielded a commonality among the behavioral structures of heat seeking, rooting, nipple grasping, and suckling that sequentially come under the control of specific characteristics of the mother. This has been demonstrated empirically in rats, for example, for sucking (Pedersen & Blass, 1982; Pedersen, Williams, & Blass, 1983). Pedersen's studies demonstrated that newborn rats' first suckling bout is determined by the odors that they experienced as fetuses being matched to odors on the mother's ventrum and nipples when the mother cleaned her infants immediately after birth by vigorously licking the anogenital region while placing the infants near her ventral surface. Normally, the initial bout is elicited by the smell of amniotic fluid deposited by the mother on her nipples (Teicher & Blass, 1977). Rats that had experienced the odor of lemon prenatally (delivered surgically to the amniotic fluid) and postnatally during anogenital stroking would *not* suckle normal nipples but would suckle washed nipples bearing lemon scent (Pedersen & Blass, 1982). Similar findings have recently been obtained in sheep (Schaal, 1993).

Later control over suckling in rats shifts to the pup's own saliva (Teicher & Blass, 1976). Pedersen et al. (1983) showed that this shift in control was caused by the mother vigorously activating her pups via anogenital stimulation in the presence of the pup saliva that coated her nipples from previous suckling episodes. Thus, sensory factors that differ from mother to mother and, given changing food availability, within a mother from season to season (mating to mating) are not specified but rather left open for the infant to discover. What appear to be specified are rules for acquiring information about these characteristics of the mother. The particular rule here is, Suckle a nipple with the odor experienced during excitation. Thus, the well-developed motor system comes under sensory control through particular experiences within the framework of a specific rule system. It is of considerable interest in this regard that anogenital stimulation in the presence of an odor causes long-term structural and functional changes in the olfactory bulb that are dependent on catecholamine release during stimulation (Leon, 1992). The behavioral and neural specializations are consonant with Marler's (1991) ideas of modular specialization, which he formulated within the context of bird song development.

Rules for governing social affiliation are not limited to suckling but extend to more general contact. Alberts (1978) has shown that odors experienced by infant rats while huddling with siblings become preferred. Even synthetic odors that have no biological significance are found attractive within the context of huddling (Alberts & Brunjes, 1978). Over time, therefore, the odors permit and elicit the motor patterns that they were originally associated with. They also cause enduring changes in motive state. Infant rats cry when separated from their dam and siblings and stop crying in the presence of a familiar odor (Oswalt & Meier, 1975). It remains to be determined whether these early sibling contacts and the attendant changes in motive state serve as a basis for later kin recognition.

These ideas have an obvious bearing on the present studies: infants for whom a stimulus has predicted either contact with the mother, the oral delivery of milk, or its natural consequences of CCK or opioid release should orient toward and prefer the predicting stimulus. This has now been demonstrated repeatedly in rats, kittens (Rosenblatt, 1983), puppies (Satinoff & Stanley, 1963), primates, and humans (Blass et al., 1984; Bushnell et al., 1983). Thus, the findings documented here of a constellation of energy-conserving changes caused by either contact or taste can independently serve as a basis for infants preferentially orienting toward (Bushnell et al., 1983; Johnson et al., 1991) and choosing to be with (Shide & Blass, 1991) the source of that change. Removal of the source is distressing (Allin & Banks, 1971; Blass et al., 1984; Noirot, 1968).

These ideas also extend the domain of embryological motor development that precedes sensory influence to the domain of motivation. We suggest that motivational systems and rules for stimulus or object selection are available at birth and await a stimulus that they can represent and seek out to sustain contact. That Bushnell et al. (1983) found a preference in 3-day-old humans for their mother's face also suggests that rudimentary cognitive structures for facial or feature recognition are available at birth and are functionally connected with motivational systems that determine preference formation and expression. If there is any validity to these ideas, they hold promise for the joint cognitive and motivational analysis of infant development.

We want to close on a speculative note concerning the implications of poorly demarcated infant motivational states in conjunction with the infant's ability to learn about those aspects of the external world that elicit different sequential motor patterns. Our working assumption is that the central changes associated with nonbounded motor expression are represented by infants as a single state of excitation rather than as specific, distinct classes of excitation. This implies that, at a later developmental stage, external stimuli associated with early excitation that occurred within a particular context (e.g., suckling) should influence behaviors (e.g., sexual behavior) that occur in contexts that differ from the original one both functionally (in terms of outcome) and structurally (in terms of the motor components of the act itself).

Fillion and Blass (1986) have presented data consonant with this view. Male rats were raised from birth until weaning (28 days) by mothers that had a lemon scent applied daily to their nipple and vaginal regions. The animals were separated from their dams after weaning and were individually housed in an isolated room for 60 days, until the time of sexual maturity. They were then allowed to mate with sexually receptive females that received the lemon scent perivaginally at the time of mating or with untreated control females. Males raised with lemon-scented females had ejaculation latencies that were about 50% shorter when mating with lemon-scented females than when mating with normal nonscented females. The converse held for normally reared control mates. Although the functional significance of shortened latencies is not known, this study makes it clear that early litter experience can have a long-term influence on a motivated behavior that is expressed for the first time only in adulthood.

More thorough documentation of the influence of nest experience on adult behavior has been presented by Holmes and Sherman (Holmes, 1988; Holmes & Sherman, 1986; Sherman, 1981) with regard to social relationships among Belding ground squirrels. Related female squirrels behave amicably among themselves and enter into alliances to protect their mutual territories, their nests, and each other's young. This recognition is determined almost entirely by nest membership during development. Thus, if natural sisters are raised in isolation from each other but with nonrelated individuals, amicable relationships are extended to nest mates, and antagonistic behaviors are directed against the "foreign" genetic sisters. For the purposes of the present exposition, we interpret this finding as implying that the characteristics of the nest mates are learned in the highly charged nest setting and that this information is later expressed in motor patterns and affiliative behaviors that either had not been expressed during the nesting period or had not been available for expression at that time.

In summary, the present studies have focused on two classes of influence that mammal mothers can use to cause changes in their infants. First, the taste of sucrose (and normally milk and fat) elicits a constellation of energy-conserving opioid- and nonopioid-mediated events. Second, these events are also caused by contact with the mother and oral stimulation by breast or pacifier. We argue that these state changes also have long-term effects on motivational processes by influencing infants' recognition of their mother and the affective intensity that she elicits (Sananes et al., 1988).

Although an explication of findings that concern early developmental influences on adult behaviors in rodents may seem remote from the human condition, we feel that the parallels between rats and humans concerning changes caused during suckling and their mediation are worth pursuing further. Nursing and suckling are evolutionarily conservative characteristics of mammals. By definition, all female mammals share the complex hormonal, physiological, and anatomical systems that permit water and nutrient sequestration from the blood in the service of milk manufacture and transfer to the infant. Infant mammals share specialized behavioral and gastrointestinal characteristics that ensure milk extraction and digestion. The suckling period is the only ontogenetic time frame characterized by ingestive and digestive commonalities because the weanling already has the ingestive and digestive specializations of adults of its species.

From our perspective, the scientific domain for understanding the short- and long-term effects of mother-infant behavioral and physiological interactions is comparative. In the same way that organ or system structure and function can be understood only through identifying morphological and functional commonalities and differences among species, so too can the behavioral structure and function of human mother-infant exchanges be understood by incorporating comparative strategies, by undertaking physiological manipulations in other animals that cannot be undertaken in research with humans, and by studying animals with relatively short life spans to appreciate the effects of early experience on later behavior. The animal findings can then provide guidelines for questions about the structure and function of human behavior and may help reveal some of the long-term influences that are determined during early development and how these may be transmitted from generation to generation. The current *Monograph* is a step in that direction.

REFERENCES

Alberts, J. R. (1978). Huddling by rat pups: Group behavioral mechanisms of temperature regulation and energy conservation. *Journal of Comparative and Physiological Psychology,* **92,** 231–240.

Alberts, J. R., & Brunjes, P. C. (1978). Ontogeny of thermal and olfactory determinants of huddling in the rat. *Journal of Comparative and Physiological Psychology,* **92,** 897–906.

Alberts, J. R., & Cramer, C. P. (1988). Ecology and experience: Sources of means and meaning of developmental change. In E. M. Blass (Ed.), *Handbook of behavioral neurobiology: Vol.* ***9.*** *Developmental psychobiology and behavioral ecology.* New York: Plenum.

Alberts, J. R., & May, B. (1984). Nonnutritive thermotactile induction of filial huddling in rat pups. *Developmental Psychobiology,* **17,** 161–181.

Allin, J. T., & Banks, E. M. (1971). Effects of temperature on ultrasound production by infant albino rats. *Developmental Psychobiology,* **4,** 149–156.

Amsel, A., Burdette, D. R., & Letz, R. (1976). Appetitive learning, patterned alteration, and extinction in 10-d-old rats with non-lactating suckling as reward. *Nature,* **262,** 816–818.

Antelman, S. M., Rowland, N. E., & Fisher, A. E. (1976). Stimulation bound ingestive behavior: A view from the tail. *Physiology and Behavior,* **17,** 743–748.

Antin, J., Gibbs, J., Holt, J., Young, R. C., & Smith, G. P. (1975). Cholecystokinin elicits the complete behavioral sequence of satiety in rats. *Journal of Comparative and Physiological Psychology,* **89,** 783–790.

Barr, R. G. (1990). The normal crying curve: What do we really know? *Developmental Medicine and Child Neurology,* **32,** 356–362.

Barr, R. G., Bakeman, R., Konner, M., & Adomson, L. (1991). Crying in Kung infants: A test of the cultural specificity hypothesis. *Developmental Medicine and Child Neurology,* **33,** 601–610.

Bateson, P. P. G. (1978). Avoiding inbreeding and optional outbreeding. *Nature,* **273,** 659–660.

Bechara, A., Harrington, F., Nader, K., & van der Kooy, D. (1992). Neurobiology of motivation: Double dissociation of two motivational mechanisms mediating opiate reward in drug-naive versus drug-dependent animals. *Behavioral Neuroscience,* **106,** 798–807.

Bernbaum, J., Pereira, G., Watkins, J., & Peckham, G. (1983). Nonnutritive sucking during gavage feeding enhances growth and maturation in premature infants. *Pediatrics,* **71,** 41–45.

Blass, E. M. (1990). Suckling: Determinants, changes, mechanisms, and lasting impressions. *Developmental Psychology,* **26**(4), 520–533.

Blass, E. M. (1992). The ontogeny of motivation: Opioid bases of energy conservation and lasting affective change in rat and human infants. *Current Directions in Psychological Science,* **1,** 116–120.

Blass, E. M. (1993). *Effect of various sugars at different concentrations on pain reactivity in newborn humans.* Manuscript in preparation.

Blass, E. M. (in press). The development of ingestive behavior: Mechanisms and implications. *Progress in Psychobiology and Physiological Psychology.*

Blass, E. M., Fillion, T. J., Rochat, P., Hoffmeyer, L. B., & Metzger, M. A. (1989). Sensorimotor and motivational determinants of hand-mouth coordination in 1–3-day old human infants. *Developmental Psychology,* **25**(6), 963–975.

Blass, E. M., Fillion, T. J., Weller, A., & Brunson, L. (1990). Separation of opioid from nonopioid mediation of affect in neonatal rats: Nonopioid mechanisms mediate maternal contact influences. *Behavioral Neuroscience,* **104**(4), 625–636.

Blass, E. M., & Fitzgerald, E. (1988). Milk-induced analgesia and comforting in 10-day-old rats: Opioid mediation. *Pharmacology, Biochemistry and Behavior,* **29,** 9–13.

Blass, E. M., Fitzgerald, E., & Kehoe, P. (1987). Interactions between sucrose, pain and isolation distress. *Pharmacology Biochemistry and Behavior,* **26,** 483–489.

Blass, E. M., Ganchrow, J. R., & Steiner, J. E. (1984). Classical conditioning in newborn humans 2–48 hours of age. *Infant Behavior and Development,* **7,** 223–235.

Blass, E. M., & Hall, W. G. (1976). Drinking termination: Interactions among hydrational, orogastric, and behavioral controls in rats. *Psychological Review,* **83,** 356–374.

Blass, E. M., & Hoffmeyer, L. B. (1991). Sucrose as an analgesic in newborn humans. *Pediatrics,* **87**(2), 215–218.

Blass, E. M., Jackson, A. M., & Smotherman, W. P. (1991). Milk-induced, opioid-mediated antinociception in rats at the time of cesarean delivery. *Behavioral Neuroscience,* **105**(5), 675–684.

Blass, E. M., & Shide, D. J. (1993). Endogenous cholecystokinin reduces vocalization in isolated 10-day-old rats. *Behavioral Neurosciences,* **107,** 304–308.

Blass, E. M., Shide, D. J., Zaw-Mon, C., & Sorentino, J. (1993). *Maternal contact suckling and analgesia in suckling rats: Evidence for nonopioid mediation.* Manuscript in preparation.

Blass, E. M., & Smith, B. A. (1992). Differential effects of sucrose, fructose, glucose and lactose on crying in 1–3-day-old human infants. *Developmental Psychology,* **28,** 804–810.

Blom, J., & Blass, E. M. (1993). *The possible role of beta-casomorphine during development in rats.* Manuscript in preparation.

Brake, S. C., Shair, H., & Hofer, M. A. (1988). Exploiting the nursing niche: The infant's sucking and feeding in the context of the mother-infant interaction. In E. M. Blass (Ed.), *Handbook of behavioral neurobiology: Vol.* **9.** *Developmental psychobiology and behavioral ecology.* New York: Plenum.

Brandl, V., & Tesmacher, H. (1979). A material with opioid activity in bovine milk and products. *Naunyn Schmiedebergs Archives Pharmacologie,* **306,** 301–304.

Brazelton, T. B. (1962). Crying in infancy. *Pediatrics,* **29,** 579–588.

Bushnell, I. W. R., Sai, F., & Mullin, J. T. (1983). Neonatal recognition of mother's face. *British Journal of Developmental Psychology,* **7,** 3–15.

Butterworth, G. (1986). Some problems in explaining the origins of movement control. In M. G. Wade & H. T. A. Whiting (Eds.), *Motor development in children: Problems of coordination and control.* Dordrecht: Nijhoff.

Campbell, B. A., & Coultier, X. (1976). The ontogenesis of learning and memory. In M. R. Rosenzweig & E. L. Bennett (Eds.), *Neural mechanisms of learning and memory.* Cambridge, MA: MIT Press.

Chiva, M. (1982). Taste, facial expression and mother-infant interaction in early development. *Baroda Journal of Nutrition,* **9,** 99–102.

Cosnier, J. (1965). *Le comportement du rat d'élevage.* Unpublished doctoral dissertation, University of Lyon, Lyon, France.

Cowart, B. J. (1981). Development of taste perception in humans: Sensitivity and preference throughout the lifespan. *Psychological Bulletin,* **90,** 43–73.

Cramer, C. P., & Blass, E. M. (1983). Rate versus volume in milk intake of suckling rats. In B. Hoebel & D. Novin (Eds.), *The neural basis of feeding and reward.* Brunswick, ME: Haer.

Cramer, C. P., Pfister, J. F., & Haig, K. A. (1988). Experience during suckling alters later spatial learning. *Developmental Psychobiology,* **21,** 1–24.

Crook, C. K. (1978). Taste perception in the newborn infant. *Infant Behavior and Development,* **1,** 52–69.

Darwin, C. (1877). A biographical sketch of an infant. *Mind,* **2,** 285–294.

DeCasper, A. J., & Fifer, W. P. (1980). Of human bonding: Newborns prefer their mothers' voices. *Science,* **208,** 1174–1176.

DeSnoo, K. (1937). Das trinkende kind im uterus. *Monatsschrift für Geburtshilfe und Gynaekologie,* **105,** 88–97.

Desor, J. A., Maller, O., & Turner, R. G. (1973). Taste in acceptance of sugars by human infants. *Journal of Comparative and Physiological Psychology,* **84,** 496–501.

Epstein, A. N., Blass, E. M., Batshaw, M. L., & Parks, A. D. (1970). The vital role of saliva as a mechanical sealant for suckling in the rat. *Physiology and Behavior,* **5,** 1395–1398.

Fentress, J. C. (1978). *Mus musicus:* The developmental orchestration of selected movement patterns in mice. In M. Bekoff & G. Burghardt (Eds.), *The development of behavior: Comparative and evolutionary aspects.* New York: Garland.

Field, T., Ignatoff, E., Stringer, S., Brennan, J., Greenberg, R., Widmayer, S., & Anderson, G. (1982). Nonnutritive sucking during tube feedings: Effects on preterm neonates in an intensive care unit. *Pediatrics,* **70,** 381–384.

Field, T., Schanberg, S. M., Scafidi, F., Bauer, C. R., Vega-Lahr, N., Garcia, R., Nystrom, J., & Kuhn, C. M. (1986). Effects of tactile/kinesthetic stimulation on preterm neonates. *Pediatrics,* **77,** 654–658.

Fillion, T. J., & Blass, E. M. (1986). Infantile experience determines adult sexual behavior in male rats. *Science,* **231,** 729–731.

Galef, B. G., Jr., & Beck, M. (1990). Diet selection and poison avoidance by mammals individually and in social groups. In E. M. Stricker (Ed.), *Handbook of behavioral neurobiology: Neurobiology of food and fluid intake* (Vol. **10**). New York: Plenum.

Galef, B. G., Jr., & Clark, M. M. (1971). Social factors in the poison avoidance and feeding behavior of wild and domesticated rat pups. *Journal of Comparative and Physiological Psychology,* **75,** 341–357.

Galef, B. G., Jr., & Sherry, D. F. (1973). Mother's milk: A medium for the transmission of cues reflecting the flavor of mother's diet. *Journal of Comparative and Physiological Psychology,* **83,** 374–378.

Glickman, S. E., & Schiff, B. (1967). A biological theory of reinforcement. *Psychological Review,* **74,** 81–109.

Gunnar, M., Fisch, R. O., & Malone, S. (1984). The effects of pacifying stimulus on behavioral and adrenocortical responses to circumcision. *Journal of the American Academy of Child Psychiatry,* **23,** 34–38.

Gubernick, D. J., & Klopfer, P. H. (1981). *Parental care in mammals.* New York: Plenum.

Hall, W. G. (1979). Feeding and behavioral activation in infant rats. *Science,* **190,** 1313–1315.

Hall, W. G. (1990). The ontogeny of ingestive behavior: Changing control of components in the feeding sequence. In E. M. Stricker (Ed.), *Handbook of behavioral neurobiology: Neurobiology of food and fluid intake* (Vol. **10**). New York: Plenum.

Hall, W. G., & Blass, E. M. (1975). Orogastric, hydrational and behavioral controls of drinking following dehydration. *Journal of Comparative and Physiological Psychology,* **89,** 939–954.

Harlow, H. F., & Harlow, M. K. (1965). The affectional systems. In A. M. Schrier, H. F. Harlow, & F. Stollnitz (Eds.), *Behavior of nonhuman primates* (Vol. **2**). New York: Academic.

Hassan, A. H., Feuerstein, G. Z., & Faden, A. I. (1982). Cardiovascular responses to opioid agonists injected into the nucleus of the tractus solitarius of unanesthetized cats. *Life Sciences,* **31,** 2193–2196.

Henning, S. J. (1981). Postnatal development: Coordination of feeding, digestion and metabolism. *American Journal of Physiology,* **241,** G199–G214.

Hofer, M. A., Shair, H., & Singh, P. (1976). Evidence that maternal ventral skin substances promote suckling in infant rats. *Physiology and Behavior,* **17,** 131–136.

Hofsten, C. von. (1984). Developmental changes in the organization of prereaching movements. *Developmental Psychology,* **20,** 378–388.

Hofsten, C. von. (1989). Arm and hand movements in the neonate. In C. von Euler (Ed.), *Neurobiology of early infant behaviour.* New York: Stockton.

Hogan, J. A. (1988). Cause and function in the development of behavior systems. In E. M. Blass (Ed.), *Handbook of behavioral neurobiology: Vol. 9. Developmental psychobiology and behavioral ecology.* New York: Plenum.

Holmes, W. G. (1988). Kinship and the development of social preferences. In E. M. Blass (Ed.), *Handbook of behavioral neurobiology: Vol. 9. Developmental psychobiology and behavioral ecology.* New York: Plenum.

Holmes, W. G., & Sherman, P. W. (1986). The ontogeny of kin recognition in two species of ground squirrels. *American Zoologist,* **22,** 491–517.

Johanson, I. B., & Hall, W. G. (1979). Appetitive learning in 1-day-old rat pups. *Science,* **205,** 419–421.

Johanson, I. B., Hall, W. G., & Polefrone, J. M. (1984). Appetitive conditioning in neonatal rats: Conditioned ingestive responding to stimuli paired with oral infusions of milk. *Developmental Psychobiology,* **17,** 357–381.

Johanson, I. B., & Teicher, M. H. (1980). Classical conditioning of an odor preference in 3-day-old rats. *Behavioral and Neural Biology,* **29,** 132–136.

Johanson, I. B., & Terry, L. M. (1988). Learning in infancy: A mechanism for behavioral change during development. In E. M. Blass (Ed.), *Handbook of behavioral neurobiology: Developmental psychobiology and behavioral ecology* (Vol. **9**). New York: Plenum.

Johnson, M. H., Dziurawiec, S., Ellis, H., & Morton, J. (1991). Newborns' preferential tracking of face-like stimuli and its subsequent decline. *Cognition,* **40,** 1–19.

Kehoe, P., & Blass, E. M. (1986a). Behaviorally functional opioid systems in infant rats: 1. Evidence for olfactory and gustatory classical conditioning. *Behavioral Neuroscience,* **100**(3), 359–367.

Kehoe, P., & Blass, E. M. (1986b). Behaviorally functional opioid systems in infant rats: 2. Evidence for pharmacological, physiological and psychological mediation of pain and stress. *Behavioral Neuroscience,* **100**(5), 624–630.

Kehoe, P., & Blass, E. M. (1986c). Central nervous system mediation of positive and negative reinforcement in neonatal albino rats. *Developmental Brain Research,* **27,** 69–75.

Kehoe, P., & Blass, E. M. (1986d). Opioid-mediation of separation distress in 10-day-old rats: Reversal of stress with maternal stimuli. *Developmental Psychobiology,* **19,** 385–398.

Kehoe, P., & Blass, E. M. (1989). Conditioned opioid release in ten-day-old rats. *Behavioural Neuroscience,* **103**(2), 423–428.

Kenny, J. T., & Blass, E. M. (1977). Suckling as an incentive to instrumental learning in preweanling rats. *Science,* **196,** 898–899.

Kiefel, J. M., Paul, D., & Bodnar, R. (1989). Reduction in opioid and non-opioid forms of swim analgesia by 5-HT2 receptor antagonists. *Brain Research,* **500,** 231–240.

Kinder, E. F. (1927). A study of nest-building activity of the albino rat. *Journal of Experimental Zoology,* **147,** 117–161.

Kleitman, N., & Satinoff, E. (1982). Thermoregulatory behavior in rat pups from birth to weaning. *Physiology and Behavior,* **29,** 537–541.

Lasiter, P. S., Wong, D. M., & Kachele, D. L. (1988). Postnatal development of the rostral solitary nucleus in rat: Dendritic morphology and mitochondrial enzyme activity. *Brain Research Bulletin,* **22,** 313–321.

Leon, M. (1992). The neurobiology of filial learning. *Annual Review of Psychology,* **43,** 377–398.

Lewis, L. D., & Williams, J. A. (1990). Regulation of cholecystokinin secretion by food, hormones and neural pathways in the rat. *American Journal of Physiology,* **258,** G512–G518.

Lipsitt, L. P. (1977). Taste in human neonates: Its effects on sucking and heart rate. In J. M. Weiffenbach (Ed.), *Taste and development: The genesis of sweet preference.* Washington, DC: U.S. Government Printing Office.

Lipsitt, L. P., & Kaye, H. (1965). Change in neonatal response to optimizing and non-optimizing sucking stimulation. *Psychonomic Science,* **2,** 331–332.

Lipsitt, L. P., Reilly, B. M., Butcher, M. J., & Greenwood, M. M. (1976). The stability and interrelationships of newborn sucking and heart rate. *Developmental Psychobiology,* **9,** 305–310.

Lorenz, K. (1943). Die angenborenen Formen moglicher Ernahrung. *Zeitschrift fur Tierpsychologie,* **5,** 235–409.

Macfarlane, A. (1975). Olfaction in the development of social preferences in the human neonate. In *Parent-infant interaction* (CIBA Foundation Symposium, no. 33). Amsterdam: Elsevier.

Maier, S. F. (1989). Determinants of the nature of environmentally induced hypoalgesia. *Behavioral Neuroscience,* **103,** 131–143.

Maller, O., & Desor, J. A. (1973). Effect of taste on ingestion by human newborns. In J. F. Bosma (Ed.), *Oral sensation and perception: Development in the fetus and infant.* Washington, DC: U.S. Government Printing Office.

Marks-Kaufman, R., Plager, A., & Kanarek, R. B. (1985). Central and peripheral contributions of endogenous opioids to nutrient selection in rats. *Psychopharmacology,* **85,** 414–418.

Marks-Kaufman, R., & Kanarek, R. B. (1981). Modifications of nutrient selection induced by naloxone in rats. *Psychopharmacology,* **74,** 321–324.

Marler, P. (1991). The instinct to learn. In S. Carey & R. Gelman (Eds.), *The epigenesis of mind: Essays on biology and cognition.* Hillsdale, NJ: Erlbaum.

Martin, W. R. (1984). Pharmacology of opioids. *Pharmacological Reviews,* **35,** 283–323.

Measel, C., & Anderson, G. (1979). Nonnutritive sucking during tube feedings: Effect on clinical course in premature infants. *Journal of Obstetrics and Gynecological and Neonatal Nursing,* **8,** 265–272.

Mistretta, C. M., & Bradley, R. M. (1988). Development of the sense of taste. In E. M. Blass (Ed.), *Handbook of behavioral neurobiology: Vol.* ***9****. Developmental psychobiology and behavioral ecology.* New York: Plenum.

Moran, T. H., Lew, M. F., & Blass, E. M. (1981). Intra-cranial self-stimulation in 3-day-old rat pups. *Science,* **214,** 1366–1368.

Moran, T. H., Sanburg, P. R., Antuoro, P. G., & Coyle, J. T. (1986). Methylazoxymethanol acetate (MAM) cortical hypoplasia alters the pattern of stimulation-induced behavior in neonatal rats. *Developmental Brain Research,* **27,** 235–242.

Moran, T. H., Schwartz, G. J., & Blass, E. M. (1983). Stimulation induced ingestion in neonatal rats. *Developmental Brain Research,* **7,** 197–204.

Morton, J., & Johnson, M. H. (1991). CONSPEC and CONLERN: A two-process theory of infant face recognition. *Psychological Review,* **98,** 164–181.

Noirot, E. (1968). Ultrasounds in small rodents: 2. Changes with age in albino rats. *Animal Behaviour,* **17,** 340–349.

Oberlander, T. F., Barr, R. G., Young, S. N., & Brian, J. A. (in press). The short-term effects of feed composition on sleeping and crying in newborn infants. *Pediatrics.*

Olson, G. A., Olson, R. D., & Kastin, A. (1987). Endogenous opiates: 1986. *Peptides,* **8,** 1135–1164.

Olson, G. A., Olson, R. D., & Kastin, A. (1989). Endogenous opiates: 1987. *Peptides,* **10,** 205–236.

Oppenheim, R. W. (1982). The neuroembryology of behavior: Progress, problems, perspectives. *Current Topics in Developmental Biology,* **17,** 257–309.

Oppenheim, R. W., & Haverkamp, L. (1986). Early development of behavior and the nervous system. In E. M. Blass (Ed.), *Handbook of behavioral neurobiology: Developmental psychobiology and developmental neurobiology* (Vol. **8**). New York: Plenum.

Oswalt, G. L., & Meier, G. W. (1975). Olfactory, thermal and tactual influences on infantile ultrasonic vocalizations in rats. *Developmental Psychobiology,* **8,** 129–135.

Pedersen, P. E., & Blass, E. M. (1982). Prenatal and postnatal determinants of the first suckling episode in albino rats. *Developmental Psychobiology,* **15,** 349–355.

Pedersen, P. E., Williams, C. L., & Blass, E. M. (1983). Activation and odor conditioning of suckling behavior in three day old albino rats. *Journal of Experimental Psychology: Animal Behavior Processes,* **8**(4), 329–341.

Pfaffmann, C. (1964). Taste, its sensory and motivating properties. *American Scientist,* **52,** 187–206.

Piaget, J. (1952). *The origins of intelligence in children* (M. Cook, Trans.). New York: International Universities Press.

Pieper, A. (1963). *The international behavioral sciences series: Cerebral function in infancy and childhood.* New York: Consultants Bureau.

Porocca, F., Mosberg, H. I., Hurst, R., Hruby, V. J., & Burks, T. F. (1984). Roles of mμ, delta and kappa opioid receptors in spinal and supraspinal mediation of gastrointestinal transit effects and hot-plate analgesia. *Journal of Pharmacology and Experimental Therapy,* **230,** 341–348.

Porter, R. H., & Moore, J. D. (1981). Human kin recognition by olfactory cues. *Physiology and Behavior,* **27,** 493–495.

Premack, D. (1962). Reversability of the reinforcement relation. *Science,* **136,** 235–237.

Punnen, S., & Sapru, H. N. (1986). Cardiovascular responses to medullary microinjections of opiate agonists in urethane-anesthetized rats. *Journal of Cardiovascular Pharmacology,* **8,** 950–956.

Rao, M., Blass, E. M., Brignol, M. J., Marino, L., & Glass, L. (1993). Effect of crying on energy metabolism of human neonates. *Pediatrics Research,* **33,** 309.

Rochat, P., Blass, E. M., & Hoffmeyer, L. B. (1988). Oropharyngeal control of hand-mouth coordination in newborn infants. *Developmental Psychology,* **24,** 459–463.

Rosenblatt, J. S. (1983). Olfaction mediates developmental transition in the altricial newborn of selected species of mammals. *Developmental Psychobiology,* **16,** 347–375.

Sameroff, A. J. (1972). Learning and adaptation in infancy: A comparison of models. In H. W. Reese (Ed.), *Advances in child development and behavior* (Vol. **7**). New York: Academic.

Sananes, C. B., Gaddy, J. R., & Campbell, B. A. (1988). Ontogeny of conditioned heart rate to an olfactory stimulus. *Developmental Psychobiology,* **21,** 117–133.

Satinoff, E., & Stanley, W. C. (1963). The effects of stomac[illegible]ading on sucking behavior in neonatal puppies. *Journal of Comparative and Physi*[illegible], **56,** 66–68.

Schaal, B. (1988). Olfaction in infants and children: Devel[illegible] functional perspectives. *Chemical Senses,* **13**(2), 145–190.

Schaal, B. (1993). Unpublished data, Laboratoire de Psycho[illegible], Centre National de Recherche Scientifique, Paris.

Schanberg, S. M., & Field, T. M. (1987). Sensory deprivation stress and supplemental stimulation in the rat pup and preterm human neonate. *Child Development,* **58**(6), 1431–1447.

Sherman, P. W. (1981). Kinship, demography, and Belding's ground squirrel nepotism. *Behavioral Ecology and Sociobiology,* **8,** 251–259.

Shide, D. J., & Blass, E. M. (1989). Opioid-like effects of intraoral infusions of corn oil and polycose on stress reactions in 10-day-old rats. *Behavioral Neuroscience,* **103**(6), 1168–1175.

Shide, D. J., & Blass, E. M. (1991). Opioid mediation of odor preferences induced by sugar and fat in 6-day-old rats. *Physiology and Behavior,* **50,** 961–966.

Smith, B. A., Fillion, T. J., & Blass, E. M. (1990). Orally-mediated sources of calming in one to three day-old human infants. *Developmental Psychology,* **26**(5), 731–737.

Spelke, E. S., Breinlinger, K., Macomber, J., & Jacobson, K. (1992). Origins of knowledge. *Psychological Review,* **99,** 605–632.

Spiers, D. E., & Adair, E. (1986). Ontogeny of homeothermy in the immature rat: Metabolic and thermal responses. *Journal of Applied Physiology,* **60,** 1190–1197.

Stainer, M. W. (1975). Effects of body weight, ambient temperature, and huddling on oxygen consumption and body temperature of young mice. *Comparative Biochemistry and Physiology,* **51A,** 79–82.

Steiner, J. E. (1979). Human facial expressions in response to taste and smell stimulation. In H. W. Reese & L. P. Lipsitt (Eds.), *Advances in child development and behavior* (Vol. **13**). New York: Academic.

Stickrod, G., Kimble, D. P., & Smotherman, W. P. (1982). Methionine 5-enkephalin effects on associations formed in utero. *Peptides,* **3,** 881–884.

Sullivan, R. M., Brake, S. C., Hofer, M. A., & Williams, C. I. (1986). Huddling and independent feeding of neonatal rats can be facilitated by a conditioned change in behavioral state. *Developmental Psychobiology,* **19,** 625–635.

Sullivan, R. M., Taborsky-Barba, S., Mendoza, R., Itano, A., Leon, M., Cotman, C. W., Payne, T. F., & Lott, I. (1991). Olfactory classical conditioning in neonates. *Pediatrics,* **87,** 511–518.

Taylor, P. M. (1960). Oxygen consumption in newborn rats. *Journal of Physiology* (London), **154,** 153–168.

Teicher, M. H., & Blass, E. M. (1976). Suckling in newborn rats: Eliminated by nipple lavage, reinstated by pup saliva. *Science,* **193,** 422–425.

Teicher, M. H., & Blass, E. M. (1977). First suckling response of the newborn albino rat: The roles of olfaction and amniotic fluid. *Science,* **198,** 635–636.

Thelen, E., & Ulrich, B. D. (1991). Hidden skills: A dynamic systems analysis of treadmill stepping during the first year. *Monographs of the Society for Research in Child Development,* **56**(1, Serial No. 223).

Valenstein, E. S., Cox, V. C., & Kakolewski, J. W. (1968). Modification of motivated behavior elicited by electrical stimulation of the lateral hypothalamus. *Science,* **159,** 1119–1120.

Weller, A., & Blass, E. M. (1988). Behavioral evidence for cholecystokinin-opiate interactions in neonatal rats. *American Journal of Physiology,* **255,** R901–R907.

Weller, A., & Blass, E. M. (1990). Cholecystokinin conditioning in rats: Ontogenetic determinants. *Behavioral Neuroscience,* **104**(1), 199–206.

Weller, A., Blass, E. M., Smith, G. P., & Gibbs, J. (1993). *Conditioned responses produced by cholecystokinin-odor pairing in neonatal rats.* Manuscript in preparation.

West, M. J., King, A. P., & Arberg, A. A. (1988). The inheritance of niches: The role of ecological legacies in ontogeny. In E. M. Blass (Ed.), *Handbook of behavioral neurobiology: Vol.* ***9****. Developmental psychobiology and behavioral ecology.* New York: Plenum.

Winslow, J. T., & Insel, T. R. (1990). Serotonergic modulation of rat pup ultrasonic vocal development: Studies with 3, 4-methylenedioxymethamphetamine. *Journal of Pharmacology and Experimental Therapeutics,* **254**(1), 212–220.

Wise, R. A., & Bozarth, M. A. (1984). Brain reward circuitry: Four circuit elements "wired" in apparent series. *Brain Research Bulletin,* **12,** 203–208.

Woodson, R., & Hamilton, C. (1986). Heart rate estimates of motor activity in preterm infants. *Infant Behavior and Development,* **9,** 283–290.

Woodson, R., & Hamilton, C. (1988). The effect of nonnutritive sucking on heart rate in preterm infants. *Developmental Psychobiology,* **21,** 207–213.

Woodson, R., Drinkwin, J., & Hamilton, C. (1985). Effects of nonnutritive sucking on state and activity. *Infant Behavior and Development,* **8,** 435–441.

ACKNOWLEDGMENTS

The studies reported in this *Monograph* were supported by a grant in aid of research (DA05724) from the National Institute for Drug and Alcohol Abuse and by a research scientist award (MH00524) from the National Institute of Mental Health to Elliott M. Blass.

We thank Kathleen Henry, Julie Ryu, and Sarah Delaney for their dedication and time in scoring the videotapes of these studies and managing the data yielded by their efforts. We also wish to acknowledge with gratitude the cooperation of Drs. Maurice Abitbol and A. J. Jain and the nursing staff at the newborn nursery of Jamaica Hospital. This study was approved by the Cornell University Committee on Human Subjects and by the Jamaica Hospital Human Subjects Committee.

Correspondence should be addressed to Elliott M. Blass, Department of Psychology, Cornell University, 248 Uris Hall, Ithaca, NY 14853.

COMMENTARY

BRIDGING SPECIES: A NEW LOOK AND NEW QUESTIONS

Ronald G. Barr

In the opening and closing pages of their *Monograph,* Blass and Ciaramitaro first raise, and then remind us, of the importance of the parallels between their studies of rats and humans for understanding behavioral structure and function, especially concerning mother-infant interaction in the preweanling period. This is appropriate. One cannot help but be impressed with the complementarity of the results of the rat studies and of the human studies reported here and in previous communications from this laboratory (e.g., Blass et al., 1989; Blass, Ganchrow, & Steiner, 1984; Blass & Hoffmeyer, 1991; Blass & Smith, 1992; Rochat, Blass, & Hoffmeyer, 1988; Smith, Fillion, & Blass, 1990). The rat studies have permitted manipulations that would be unethical in humans and that help demonstrate mechanisms; the human studies have provided confirmatory analogues and extended the significance of the rat studies to a species that even the most uninterested reader of the animal literature can hardly ignore. While such bridging of species is often the "promissory note" of nonhuman studies, the promise is not so often fulfilled, and rarely from the same laboratory. Whether one comes from the "animal" or the "human" side of behavioral studies, I suspect that most readers of this *Monograph* will have at least entertained the thought—perhaps even dreamed a little—about opening up a parallel laboratory across the hall to share the sort of excitement that bridging species in this way can bring.

Furthermore, the topic of the studies is clearly of general interest. The authors argue (1) that, in the feeding act, mothers affect their infant's behavior in at least two ways (through orotactile and orogustatory stimulation); (2) that each form of stimulation is mediated by different neural pathways;

(3) that the orogustatory stimulation is mediated centrally by endogenous opioids; (4) that, by providing these forms of stimulation and engaging these mechanisms, the feeding act thereby affects state, heart rate, activity level, eye opening, and hand-mouth coordination, providing a means of influencing energy conservation, growth, motivation, and learning; and (5) that these influences are likely to persist long after the breast-feeding phase has been completed. It is an impressive synthesis. It is difficult to imagine that the argument does not impinge at some point on the field of interest of almost any student of behavior, growth, and development, whatever his or her background or theoretical perspective.

Of course, not all the points in my summary of Blass and Ciaramitaro's presentation are treated in the same detail or with the same kind of argumentation. The evidence supporting each point derives variably from a broadly based literature with particular reference to psychobiological studies of mother-infant interaction, from the previous studies of rats and humans in the authors' own laboratory, and from the new empirical data on human infants presented for the first time in this *Monograph*. Allowing for some simplification, what stands out for me as new in the new data are the following:

1. There is a substantial replication of previous findings from this laboratory concerning the effects (and the time course of the effects) of sucrose and pacifiers on calming crying infants and eliciting hand-mouth contact.

2. The distinction and comparison between the effects of sucrose in "agitated" and "calm" normal newborn infants also stands out. In most previous studies, Blass and his colleagues had looked at groups of "spontaneously crying" infants, which meant that the infants may or may not have been crying at the time the sucrose was delivered. Here, the infants are split into two groups. This permits us to see whether the effects are there when infants are "really crying" and whether the effects on the various outcome measures are state dependent. Given the now substantial literature on the importance of behavioral state as an organizing principle of infant behavior and the nonlinearity of response depending on state (e.g., Korner, 1972; Nijhuis et al., 1982; Prechtl & O'Brien, 1982; Wolff, 1987), one might have expected some differences, and there were.

3. In comparison to previous studies, three outcome measures were added—heart rate, gross motor activity, and eye opening—that add to our understanding of the generality of, the differences in, and the interaction of the effects of sucrose and pacifier. In addition, heart rate and motor activity provide some proxy measures for decreased energy utilization, and eye opening may be relevant to the infant's learning about the caregiver delivering the stimulus.

4. The demonstrated combined effects of sucrose and pacifier begin to put the elements of the orogustatory and orotactile stimulation back to-

gether, bringing the laboratory analogue closer to the real-life situation that it was designed to resemble.

5. The finding of sucrose and pacifier effects in the four infants of methadone-treated mothers is important evidence that functioning endogenous opioid systems are required for the sucrose effects but not the pacifier effects. It is the best evidence yet not only that the behavioral effects of sucrose have important parallels in the infant rat and human studies but also that the underlying mechanisms may be parallel as well.

6. The findings of the case report of the infant of a methadone-treated mother—in whom a daily 30-min pacifier-sucking intervention was associated with stabilization (the authors prefer "reduction") of caloric intake in the presence of continuing weight gain—are consistent with the suggestion of energy conservation in the presence of nonnutritive sucking and raise the ante in favor of a more systematic study that would control other possible influences that could be accounting for, or contributing to, this result.

In the remarks that follow, I will concentrate primarily on these new observations. This is not to discount or underestimate the importance or value of the broader context of the work into which these studies were so articulately put but only to provide a focus on what is unique to the *Monograph.*

The primary claim that these studies are concerned to support is that there are two independent systems of state regulation accessible via oral mechanisms but mediated by different neural pathways. By and large, the reported findings are consistent with and support that claim. In addition, as any good set of observations should, the findings raise interesting new questions, many of which should be amenable to experimental verification. Those that occur to me fall roughly into two categories: questions arising from the interpretation and significance of the results for the immediate aims of the study itself and questions about the significance of the findings for the broader context of mother-infant interaction in normal contexts, for which these studies are "analogues."

Implications for the Interpretation of the Study Results

Temporal Characteristics of the Response to Sucrose and Pacifier

A key to the argument made for the effects of sucrose (taste, orogustatory stimuli) and pacifier (contact, orotactile stimuli) being mediated by different systems is that the time courses (sometimes referred to as the "operating characteristics") of the effects are different. Pacifier effects are characterized as being immediate, on-off, or square wave-like effects, sucrose effects as being gradual in onset and offset, or ramp-like effects. The importance of focusing on time-course differences is understandable since the effects are otherwise very similar and one is restricted from performing pharmacologic intervention studies on human infants. Time-course information can be tricky, however, because it can be affected by so many determinants, including the way the experiment is set up. Consequently, one interesting question concerns the extent to which the time-course differences are a function of the type of stimulus or of the experimental paradigm.

Bear in mind that the characteristics of the experimental paradigm are that an infant receives repeated administrations of sucrose (or water) once per minute for 10 sec per minute over 5 min by syringe, or the same once per minute for 1 min by pacifier. In addition, the temporal characteristics are reported on the basis of 1-min intervals. A number of elements of the paradigm might predispose toward an on-off time course with pacifier and a ramp time course with sucrose. Examination of these might raise some interesting questions about how robust the temporal characteristics are and what they mean without, I think, altering the essential claim of the argument.

1. The stimuli are not equivalent not only with regard to whether they are tactile or gustatory (which is appropriate since that is what is being tested) but also with regard to the extent to which they "block" incompatible behaviors such as crying. The authors are sensitive to this incompatibility and suggest that the other measures should not be so constrained. However, crying—both in fact and for purposes of the study—is not simply a "vocal act" but a state of the organism. Consequently, the "blocking" effect of pacifiers does, and should, extend to measures of activity, heart rate, hand-mouth contact, and even, arguably, eye opening.

2. The stimuli may not be equivalent with regard to the sufficiency of the dose of contact or taste. Thus, for example, a more concentrated or greater "taste" dose might produce a more immediate "on" effect, one similar to that of the pacifier.

3. The stimuli may not be equivalent with regard to salience of contact or taste. This is almost impossible to judge, of course, especially across perceptual systems for which there is no "common currency" (as there is for comparisons between tastes, e.g.). In principle, however, a more salient stimulus might produce a more acute "on" effect even for tastes.

4. Because the time course of the effects is reported in 1-min blocks, more rapid short-term effects of taste that were not sustained for 1 min would be less apparent when averaged over each minute. This would not occur with the pacifier because it remained in place for the whole of each minute.

5. The repeated stimuli may differentially affect the offset of the taste versus contact stimuli related to the continuing (or lingering) presence of the stimulus in the mouth. This might "build up" in the case of taste and

persist beyond the fifth treatment minute, which would not be the case for pacifier stimulation.

6. The offset may be affected by the fact that, whereas the pacifier is withdrawn at the end of the fifth minute, the removal of the sucrose is more gradual and dampened by the continuing intraoral taste. It is not clear how much of the sharper increase in agitation following pacifier removal is due to the absence of continued stimulation, the rapidity of the change from stimulation to no stimulation, or the "frustration" induced by the act of withdrawing the pacifier.

Whether any or all of these might be contributing to the differences in time-course characteristics remains speculation, although many would be amenable to empirical test.

Stimulated in part by the work of Blass and his colleagues, my colleagues and I have examined the effects of gustatory stimuli in crying infants in a slightly different paradigm. In our procedure, infants are observed after diaper changing until they cry continuously for 15 consecutive sec, at which time 250 μl of solution is delivered once and the infants are observed for up to 5 min (or 2 consecutive min of crying). The time course is reported in 10-sec intervals.

The main findings have provided an independent replication of the observations of Blass and his colleagues. First, sucrose produces a substantial calming effect represented by 60% less crying relative to water throughout the 5-min observation period (Barr et al., in press). Second, the relative time courses of crying reduction, mouthing, and hand-mouth contact effects are essentially the same as reported by Blass et al. (1989; see also Fig. 1 of this *Monograph*); that is, crying cessation lasted well beyond sucrose administration, mouthing behavior increased to a peak within 10 sec and then decreased rapidly during the next 2 min, and increased hand-mouth contact was constantly elevated for about 2 min.

These findings may also contribute to the questions about the time-course characteristics of crying response. First, they demonstrate that the prolonged postsucrose effect does not depend on repeated administrations since the difference with water persisted for at least 5 min. This makes the problem noted in point 5 above arguably less likely, although the question of persisting taste with even one administration cannot be ruled out. Second, with this dose, the effect was immediate, dropping to 10% in the first 10 sec, but averaging about 15% (9 sec per minute) over the first 2 min. Thereafter, crying tended to increase under both sucrose and water conditions but continued to remain substantially lower for sucrose throughout the observation period. This suggests that 250 μl of 24% sucrose is more salient and/or sufficient to produce an immediate "on" response.

In a second study, we tested the effect of 250 μl of 0.25% quinine HCl solution against water and sucrose (Graillon et al., 1993a). Quinine solution is interesting because it is a salient taste for newborns but aversive, producing a typical "disgust" face reaction when given to calm newborns (Rosenstein & Oster, 1988; Steiner, 1977). However, when given to crying newborns, it produced a rapid (i.e., within 10 sec) calming effect, but one that lasted for only 1 min (relative to water), was not as strong as sucrose, and did not increase hand-mouth contact.

Relative to the points about time course, these studies suggest that many gustatory stimuli, whether hedonically positive or aversive, may produce an immediate effect on crying. However, the more gradual prolonged offset of sucrose seems more robust and less susceptible to differences in experimental procedure. The elicitation of hand-mouth contact by sucrose but not quinine contributes to the argument that different systems may be accessed by these two salient tastes. A possible interpretation of these results and those of Blass and his colleagues is that the initial phase of quieting (lasting about 1 min, as suggested by the quinine results) relates to "attention" to salient gustatory stimuli (which may be dose dependent) while the second phase of prolonged calm specific to sucrose relates to access to opioid-dependent central systems. This would be consistent with the description of delayed onset provided by Blass and Ciaramitaro. Interestingly, the "flurry of activity" in the initial placing of the pacifier might represent the analogue of the initial "attention" phase for orotactile stimuli as well.

Of course, it could be argued that, even if the two experimental stimuli are not equivalent with regard to incompatible response, sufficiency of dose, salience, and so on, neither are they equivalent in real life. What may be more important is that the experimental paradigm is close to the natural feeding situation. However, the extent to which the experimental time-course characteristics reflect real-life time-course characteristics is also uncertain. For example, is it the case that milk is available to the oral cavity only in 10 sec per minute bursts, or is the mouth constantly "awash" with milk during a feeding bout?

Do Pacifiers and/or Sucrose Cause a State Change?

Explicitly, the authors are interested in knowing whether orotactile and/or orogustatory stimuli (particularly sucrose) cause a change in state and whether the effects of the stimuli are state dependent. However, although the concept of behavioral state can be understood qualitatively and utilized as a major organizing principle of infant (especially newborn) behavior (e.g., Korner, 1972; Nijhuis et al., 1982; Prechtl, 1974; Prechtl & O'Brien, 1982; Wolff, 1987), it tends to resist precise definition.

One feature of the concept is that the variables that are taken as indices of behavioral state are presumed to represent an organizational characteristic of the whole organism. However, no one motor variable defines the state of the organism. If one part of the pattern of activity that we think of as the crying state (say, gross motor activity) is not occurring, that may be because the state has changed or because that particular behavior is not able to be expressed. Thus, if the infant were swaddled but still producing regular, cyclic negative vocalizations, we would probably consider the infant still to be in a crying state. A second feature of the concept is that there is some stability of states, meaning that they persist over time and are relatively resistant to perturbation. Thus, if an infant is in a crying state before being stimulated (with taste or contact, e.g.) but returns to crying after the stimulus is removed, was the state "changed," or did the stimulus simply "perturb" the state temporarily, with the organism reorganizing itself to a crying state? A third feature is that the infant will respond differently, and in a nonlinear way, depending on which state he or she is in when stimulated.

Blass and Ciaramitaro's (and our) studies provide some good examples of the third feature, namely, the nonlinear, state-dependent response. They report, for example, that activity was reduced in response to sucrose and pacifier when the infants were crying ("agitated") but did not change when they were calm. Notably, hand-mouth contact occurred following sucrose stimulation only when crying, not when calm. Similarly, sucrose and pacifier moved infants from crying to calm but not from calm to sleep. Our studies with quinine produced a rather striking example too: quinine produces a "disgust" face when given to quiet infants but a calm, attentive face when given to crying infants (Graillon et al., 1993a).

However, the significance of the first and second features of the state concept is less easy to interpret and more problematic. It seems to be so for Blass and Ciaramitaro as well. For example, in the discussion section of Chapter III, they take it as demonstrated that "each system . . . can independently reverse state in agitated infants" (p. 36). Earlier, however, when comparing the results of pacifiers that were treated with water or sucrose, they suggest that "stimulation of the oral cavity with a pacifier quiets but does not cause a *fundamental* state change" (p. 31; my emphasis). Similarly, they take the absence of posttreatment differences in activity level to argue that activity was controlled by pacifier stimulation and "did not reflect a *fundamental* state change" (p. 33; my emphasis). Thus, they seem to draw a distinction between state change and fundamental state change: the former seems to be more like a perturbation after which the system "rights itself" and returns quickly to crying; the latter seems to be a "true" state change, primarily because the noncrying state endures beyond the time of the stimulation.

I think (although I am not sure that the authors would agree with this interpretation) that Blass and Ciaramitaro are suggesting that orotactile stimulation (or at least pacifier stimulation) only perturbs the crying state while orogustatory stimulation actually changes it, despite their later statement about both systems changing state. Consequently, the appeal to stability (feature 2) becomes an appeal to time course. The fact that the behaviors typical of crying cease for 5 min during pacifier stimulation need not mean that the state has been changed since those behaviors are not necessarily defining of the state of the organism and reexpress themselves as soon as the stimulation ceases (feature 1).

Consequently, it seems that, intentionally or not, Blass and Ciaramitaro have raised a difficult question about the concept of infant state. If one asks, Do pacifiers and/or sucrose change infant state? one's ability to answer that question may indicate more about what one means by the concept of infant state than about what one knows of the quieting effects of pacifiers or sucrose.

Ultimately, an appeal to time course—although understandable—will not, I think, be satisfactory. First, the time course of the behavioral changes is logically neutral to the question of organismic state change. There is no a priori reason why any one scale of time more than another should be used to define state change. Second, it follows that any imposed criterion will be arbitrary. For example, Prechtl and O'Brien (1982, p. 6) suggested that "at least one, often preferably three, minutes" be included in a moving window for assessing state transitions. Under this criterion, all the infants in the pacifier and sucrose groups would have experienced a true state change. In our single sucrose stimulus study (Barr et al., in press), we can represent subject response individually by means of a "survival analysis curve." Although the group mean crying was 60% lower for sucrose than water throughout the 5-min observation period, reattainment of at least 15 consecutive sec of crying (which virtually always continued for 2 min) occurred in 20% of infants by 1 min, 35% of infants by 3 min, and 65% of infants by 5 min. How many of those infants should we say experienced a "state change"? Third, as noted previously, time-course parameters are often subject to design factors that have the potential to make significant contributions in addition to those of the system directly under investigation.

The answer, if there is one, may require a redefinition of the state concept. Wolff, who has written articulately on this subject (Wolff, 1987), suggests that states will need to be understood in terms of "coherence" among sets of variables (such as negative vocalizations, gross motor activity, heart rate, etc.) rather than as sets of specific values that the variables have at any point in time. An appropriate coherence measure would have the characteristic of capturing the relation between the subsystems that are "assembled" to form a state that has stability or "disassembled" during transitions to other states. It would function very much like the measure of phase relations of limbs so successfully utilized by Thelen and her colleagues in studies of development of infant limb movements (e.g., Thelen, 1989;

Thelen & Ulrich, 1991). In principle, quantitative changes in the variables describing the subsystems would bring about qualitative changes from one state to another, represented by discontinuous changes in the coherence measure. A true state change would be indicated by the measure of coherence rather than by an arbitrary decision as to whether sucrose or pacifier effects lasted 1 or 3 min.

To be sure, such an approach remains a promissory note since such coherence measures remain to be defined—a nontrivial problem. This is likely to be an even more difficult task for highly complex organized systems like infant states than it is for limb movements. Nevertheless, the impetus and potential value of the pursuit of such measures is underlined by the problems of state definition and the attempt to understand the caregiver's role in state regulation via these orogustatory and orotactile stimuli and the mechanisms that they engage.

Infants of Methadone-Maintained Mothers

In light of the above potential difficulties with temporal measures of the responses to sucrose and pacifier and temporal criteria for state changes, the report of the infants born to mothers maintained on methadone during pregnancy is of critical importance (see Chap. IV). As the authors point out, the predictions are clear cut, and these observations represent the best evidence yet of the independence of the two mechanisms underlying orogustatory and orotactile stimuli. Because there has been an "intervention" predictably specific to one of the two proposed underlying mechanisms, the evidence is not entirely dependent on the time course of the response. The responses of the described infant are impressive and speak to the importance of detailed descriptions of even very few subjects in special circumstances. In light of their importance, one would have been happy to see the detailed results from all four infants. These fascinating results will ensure that the subsequent comprehensive report will be eagerly anticipated.

Implications for the Natural Context

Will the Results with Sucrose Extend to Breast Milk?

Understandably, Blass and his colleagues have exploited and continue to exploit the remarkable opportunities that sucrose provides for elucidating the operating characteristics of the presumably opioid-mediated state regulation system accessed by taste (flavor). Sucrose is the most effective of the carbohydrates tested to date (Blass & Smith, 1992) and has the additional methodological advantage of being without smell, a potential confound in taste studies. However, it is a virtually unquestioned assumption that the results will extend to the natural mother-infant breast-feeding situation. The assumption is not unreasonable. At least with rat pups, milk formula, corn oil, and polycose all have similar opioid-antagonist reversible effects in pain and separation stress experimental paradigms (Blass & Fitzgerald, 1988; Blass, Jackson, & Smotherman, 1991; Shide & Blass, 1989). If fats work also, then breast milk would provide two categories of nutrients that might access the system.

Still, there may be a few reasons to be looking forward to a direct demonstration of parallel findings in normal human infants in response to breast milk. One is that not all mechanisms underlying nutrient-behavior relations demonstrated to be present in rats transfer to naturalistic human infant contexts. For example, dietary recruitment of centrally mediated synthesis of serotonin has been well demonstrated in rats and humans (Fernstrom & Wurtman, 1971; Young & Gauthier, 1981), and increased tryptophan ingestion (the serotonin precursor) produces reduced latency to sleep and increased drowsiness in adults (Hartmann & Greenwald, 1984; Spring, Chido, & Bowen, 1987). Strikingly similar results in sleep latency and duration had been described in newborns when fed combined tryptophan and carbohydrate "meals" (Yogman & Zeisel, 1983). It therefore seemed reasonable to suppose that these mechanisms would contribute to state regulation in newborns under typical feeding conditions.

We designed a direct test of this assumption in which three groups of infants were randomized to receive a water, lactose, or balanced formula feeding and infant state was recorded for 40 min postprandially (Oberlander et al., 1992). The results were surprising to some extent, and some are relevant to the work reported in this *Monograph.* First, the assumption that dietary recruitment of central serotonergic systems would affect behavior in normal feeding situations was not supported. On the basis of the underlying physiology, earlier and more postprandial sleep would be predicted with a "lactose meal" than with a balanced formula meal, but the opposite turned out to be the case (Oberlander et al., 1992). This suggests that, although available, other mechanisms recruited by milk ingestion are more important or "override" any effects due to dietary recruitment of the serotonergic system. Second, consistent with the "prototypical setting" described by Blass and Ciaramitaro, the greatest period of noncrying wakefulness occurred in the first 10 min following feeding, providing an opportunity for interaction that responsive parents could exploit. Third, however, was the fact that the amount of wakefulness was not related to the type of meal ingested (even water was as effective as either nutrient group), suggesting that wakefulness was determined more by the act of feeding than by the food itself. Consequently, even well-established mechanisms in animal models may or may not be demonstrated to be determinants when examined in real-life, or at least naturalistic, caretaking settings.

In addition, however, it is striking and apparently paradoxical that such a dramatic effect on infant state can be produced by sucrose when sucrose is not a constituent of human breast milk, or for that matter of the milk of almost all other mammalian species. Interestingly, lactose is the predominant carbohydrate in human breast milk, constituting 70%–80% of total carbohydrate, in concentrations of 5.6%–6.9% (weight/volume) in the first 4 months of life (Coppa et al., 1993). It has been shown (Blass & Smith, 1992) to be significantly less effective than sucrose in calming newborns when given in comparable doses. Moreover, if sweetness is the operative dimension of the carbohydrate effect, a 6% lactose concentration would (to adults) be approximately equivalent in sweetness to a 2.4% sucrose solution (Gusry & Secretin, 1991). Even in rat pups, the effectiveness of milk formula in reducing separation-induced distress vocalizations was not apparent until 2 min after infusion, which might imply that its effectiveness is post- rather than preingestive (Blass & Fitzgerald, 1988).

If sweetness is the operative dimension, then the effectiveness of lactose might be increased by its combination with fat in breast milk. Alternatively, the fat content of milk might access the system at the oral level independently (Shide & Blass, 1989). However, we recently found no effect of corn oil in calming newborn infants using our paradigm (Graillon et al., 1993b). Perhaps most interesting, we also found no effect of expressed breast milk (colostrum) in a pilot study of 1–3-day-old newborn infants (unpublished observations). Whether this lack of effect will be replicated and/or extend to more mature milk remains to be determined, of course. The story, as Alice said in Wonderland, gets curiouser and curiouser.

Role of Opioid Systems in Normal Caregiving

In their description of the "prototypic setting" in which mothers might feed their infants, Blass and Ciaramitaro note that mothers usually employ contact and/or nursing. As a result, they propose that the "stimuli that predict state changes [produced by these events] acquire enduring affective significance" (p. 3). They later argue persuasively that such associations provide the infant with a potentially remarkable set of learning and motivational experiences. Because feeding is a frequent act in mother-infant interchanges, it provides many iterations of such motivational-learning opportunities.

Assuming for the moment that breast-feeding does in fact engage these mechanisms, the potential significance of this bears underlining, I think, for a couple of reasons. First, if feeding provides many such opportunities in contemporary Western society, it provides even more in other societies where the breast-feeding interval is even shorter (e.g., Konner, 1972; Lozoff & Brittenham, 1979). For example, !Kung San hunter-gatherers feed approximately 4 times per hour for 1–2 min each time for the first 2 or 3 years of life (Konner & Worthman, 1980). Second, while it is widely accepted that early infant crying may well function to assure adequate nutrition and biological needs, it is less widely appreciated that positive verbal social interaction is associated with caretaker response as well. In fact, in studies that have documented the "package" of caregiving responses to infant cries, social behaviors (such as talking, smiling, singing, etc.) have been prominent, in some cases even more prominent, than feeding and contact (Barr, 1990; Bell & Ainsworth, 1972; Gustafson & DeConti, 1990; Gustafson & Harris, 1990; Konner, 1972; Moss, 1974). In fact, cries may function positively as the beginning of "verbal dialogues" in early infancy. To the extent that these verbal dialogues are associated with opioid-mediated feeding and calming, crying might arguably be recruiting a biological predisposition for later language learning as well.

Third, if these arguments concerning motivation and learning experience are true, it might be of interest to ask what the effect may be of the differences in caretaking between current Western practice and that thought to be typical of our evolutionary past as represented by current hunter-gatherer practice. Cross-cultural comparisons suggest that there have been some shifts in the extent to which social interaction and feeding are associated. In the !Kung San hunter-gatherers, for example, the probability that an infant will nurse within 15 sec of a cry/fret event is about 40% and that the mother will provide a verbal social response about 30% (Barr et al., 1987), and the two most often occur as part of a "package" (Barr, 1990). In contemporary Western caregiving, social interaction associated with feeding in response to crying occurs less than 20% of the time, and social responses alone are predominant (about 65%) (Gustafson & DeConti, 1990). This suggests that language stimuli are becoming relatively dissociated from feeding context and the potential connection with opioid stimulation.

Implications for Further Interdisciplinary Studies

One cannot leave the issue of the potential significance of these studies without at least a note about the implications for the study of behavior both within and across disciplines. As a physician, I could not help noticing that

Blass and Ciaramitaro's statement "the behavioral consequences of receiving milk have remained largely unexplored" (p. 4) could not possibly have been written by a pediatrician. Of course, it was written in the context of the comparison with the attention paid to contact in child development and psychology, where the contrast is probably appropriate. In pediatrics, if anything, the situation is the reverse: undue attention has been paid to the effect of milk on behavior (especially in relation to the clinical syndrome of excessive crying, or "colic") and insufficient attention to behavioral determinants (see, e.g., Barr, 1991a; Miller & Barr, 1991).

Their statement does hold true for pediatrics in another sense, however. By and large, the interest in milk and behavior has been focused on whether the intake of breast-feeding mothers is abnormally low (insufficient milk syndrome) or whether ingested milk or formula produces abnormal hypersensitivity reactions to milk protein or malabsorption of milk sugars—in short, whether ingested milk produces pathophysiological responses. If abnormal physiological responses are not implicated, physicians tend to abandon the field and assume that the answers will be found in the breakdown of mother-infant interactions or affective problems. This work by Blass and Ciaramitaro should remind us that mother-infant behavioral interactions are most likely mediated by normal physiological interactions that, furthermore, may be very germane to how much an infant cries. Given that pathology probably accounts for less than 5% of colic in infants (Miller & Barr, 1991), attention to *normal* physiological mechanisms recruited by the feeding act might be a productive endeavor even in the investigation of behavioral clinical syndromes (Barr, 1991b).

I expect, however, that the implicit message of this *Monograph* is the same regardless of field of training: namely, our understanding will be richer if we can discourse fluently in at least two "languages" at the same time in the same study. After having read the *Monograph,* I find it difficult to imagine that I would really understand what was going on in a breast-feeding interaction without being aware of milk constituents, taste, and opioids no matter how detailed the behavioral description or that I would really understand the importance of milk constituents and opioids without being aware of how they affected behavior no matter how fine the chemical or physiological description. This *Monograph* is an eloquent testament to the value of these sorts of psychobiological studies. It reminds us that these questions can be asked and systematically investigated and goes a long way toward answering them.

References

Barr, R. G. (1990). The early crying paradox: A modest proposal. *Human Nature,* **1,** 355–389.

Barr, R. G. (1991a). Colic and gas. In W. A. Walker, P. R. Durie, J. R. Hamilton, J. A. Walker-Smith, & J. G. Watkins (Eds.), *Pediatric gastrointestinal disease: Pathophysiology, diagnosis and management.* Burlington, VT: Decker.

Barr, R. G. (1991b, June). *Explaining illness by normal biobehavioral interactions: An hypothesis.* Paper presented at the conference "Environment-Illness Interaction," Center for Human Development and Developmental Disabilities, Robert Wood Johnson Medical School, New Brunswick, N.J.

Barr, R. G., Bakeman, R., Konner, M., & Adamson, L. (1987). Crying in !Kung infants: Distress signals in a responsive context [Abstract]. *American Journal of Diseases in Children,* **141,** 386.

Barr, R. G., Quek, V., Cousineau, D., Oberlander, T. F., Brian, J. A., & Young, S. N. (in press). Effects of intraoral sucrose on crying, mouthing and hand-mouth contact in newborn and six-week old infants. *Developmental Medicine and Child Neurology.*

Bell, S. M., & Ainsworth, D. S. (1972). Infant crying and maternal responsiveness. *Child Development,* **43,** 1171–1190.

Blass, E. M., Fillion, T. J., Rochat, P., Hoffmeyer, L. B., & Metzher, M. A. (1989). Sensorimotor and motivational determinants of hand-mouth coordination in 1–3-day-old human infants. *Developmental Psychology,* **25,** 963–975.

Blass, E. M., & Fitzgerald, E. (1988). Milk-induced analgesia and comforting in 10-day-old rats: Opioid mediation. *Pharmacology, Biochemistry and Behavior,* **29,** 9–13.

Blass, E. M., Ganchrow, J. R., & Steiner, J. E. (1984). Classical conditioning in newborn humans 2–48 hours of age. *Infant Behavior and Development,* **7,** 223–235.

Blass, E. M., & Hoffmeyer, L. B. (1991). Sucrose as an analgesic for newborn infants. *Pediatrics,* **87,** 215–218.

Blass, E. M., Jackson, A. M., & Smotherman, W. P. (1991). Milk-induced, opioid-mediated antinociception in rats at the time of cesarean delivery. *Behavioral Neuroscience,* **105**(5), 677–686.

Blass, E. M., & Smith, B. A. (1992). Differential effects of sucrose, fructose, glucose, and lactose on crying in 1- to 3-day-old human infants: Qualitative and quantitative considerations. *Developmental Psychology,* **28**(5), 804–810.

Coppa, G. V., Gabrielli, O., Pierani, P., Catassi, C., Carlucci, A., & Giorgi, P. L. (1993). Changes in carbohydrate composition in human milk over 4 months of lactation. *Pediatrics,* **91**(3), 637–641.

Fernstrom, J. D., & Wurtman, R. J. (1971). Brain serotonin content: Increase following ingestion of a carbohydrate diet. *Science,* **174,** 1023–1025.

Graillon, A., Barr, R. G., Young, S. N., Wright, J. H., & Hendricks, L. A. (1993a). Calming crying newborns with sucrose: Is the effect specific to sweet taste? [Abstract]. *Pediatric Research,* **33**(4, pt. 2), 11A.

Graillon, A., Barr, R. G., Young, S. N., Wright, J. H., & Hendricks, L. A. (1993b). *Calming crying newborns with sucrose: Is the effect specific to sweet taste?* Manuscript in preparation.

Gusry, P. R., & Secretin, M. C. (1991). Sugars and nonnutritive sweeteners. In M. Gracey, N. Kretchmer, & E. Rossi (Eds.), *Sugars in nutrition: Nestle Nutrition Workshop series.* New York: Raven.

Gustafson, G. E., & DeConti, K. A. (1990). Infants' cries in the process of normal development. *Early Child Development and Care,* **65,** 45–56.

Gustafson, G. E., & Harris, K. L. (1990). Women's responses to young infants' cries. *Developmental Psychology,* **26,** 144–152.

Hartmann, E., & Greenwald, D. (1984). Tryptophan and human sleep: An analysis of 43 studies. In H. G. Schlossberger, W. Kochen, B. Linzen, & H. Steinhart (Eds.), *Progress in tryptophan and serotonin research.* New York: de Gruyter.

Konner, M. J. (1972). Aspects of the developmental ethology of a foraging people. In N. G. Blurton-Jones (Ed.), *Ethological studies of child behavior.* Cambridge: Cambridge University Press.

Konner, M. J., & Worthman, C. (1980). Nursing frequency, gonadal function, and birth spacing among !Kung hunter-gatherers. *Science,* **207,** 788–791.

Korner, A. F. (1972). State as variable, as obstacle, and as mediator of stimulation in infant research. *Merrill-Palmer Quarterly,* **18,** 77–94.

Lozoff, B., & Brittenham, G. (1979). Infant care: Cache or carry. *Journal of Pediatrics,* **95,** 478–483.

Miller, A. R., & Barr, R. G. (1991). Infantile colic: Is it a gut issue? *Pediatric Clinics of North America,* **38**(6), 1407–1423.

Moss, H. A. (1974). Communication in mother-infant interaction. In L. Krames, P. Pliner, & T. Alloway (Eds.), *Nonverbal communication.* New York: Plenum.

Nijhuis, J. G., Prechtl, H. F. R., Martin, C. B., Jr., & Bots, R. S. G. M. (1982). Are there behavioural states in the human fetus? *Early Human Development,* **6,** 177–195.

Oberlander, T. F., Barr, R. G., Young, S. N., & Brian, J. A. (1992). Short-term effects of feed composition on sleeping and crying in newborn infants. *Pediatrics,* **90**(5), 733–740.

Prechtl, H. F. R. (1974). The behavioural states of the newborn infant (a review). *Brain Research,* **76,** 185–212.

Prechtl, H. F. R., & O'Brien, M. J. (1982). Behavioural states of the full-term newborn: The emergence of a concept. In P. Stratton (Ed.), *Psychobiology of the human newborn.* New York: Wiley.

Rochat, P., Blass, E. M., & Hoffmeyer, L. B. (1988). Oropharyngeal control of hand-mouth coordination in newborn infants. *Developmental Psychology,* **24,** 459–463.

Rosenstein, D., & Oster, H. (1988). Differential facial responses to four basic tastes in newborns. *Child Development,* **59,** 1555–1568.

Shide, D. J., & Blass, E. M. (1989). Opioidlike effects of intraoral infusions of corn oil and polycose on stress reactions in 10-day-old rats. *Behavioral Neuroscience,* **103,** 1168–1175.

Smith, B. A., Fillion, T. J., & Blass, E. M. (1990). Orally mediated sources of calming in 1 to 3-day old human infants. *Developmental Psychology,* **26,** 731–737.

Spring, B., Chido, J., & Bowen, D. J. (1987). Carbohydrates, tryptophan, and behavior: A methodological review. *Psychological Bulletin,* **102,** 234–256.

Steiner, J. E. (1977). Facial expressions of the neonate infant indicating the hedonics of food-related chemical stimuli. In J. M. Weiffenbach (Ed.), *Taste and development: The genesis of sweet preference.* Bethesda, MD: U.S. Department of Health, Education and Welfare.

Thelen, E. (1989). Self-organization in developmental processes: Can systems approaches work? In M. R. Gunnar & E. Thelen (Eds.), *Systems and development: The Minnesota Symposia on Child Psychology.* Hillsdale, NJ: Erlbaum.

Thelen, E., & Ulrich, B. D. (1991). Hidden skills: A dynamic systems analysis of treadmill stepping during the first year. *Monographs of the Society for Research in Child Development,* **56**(1, Serial No. 223).

Wolff, P. H. (1987). *The development of behavioral states and the expression of emotions in early infancy: New proposals for investigation.* Chicago: University of Chicago Press.

Yogman, M. W., & Zeisel, S. H. (1983). Diet and sleep patterns in newborn infants. *New England Journal of Medicine,* **309,** 1147–1149.

Young, S. N., & Gauthier, S. (1981). Effect of tryptophan administration on tryptophan, 5-hydroxyindoleacetic acid and indoleacetic acid in human lumar and cisternal cerebrospinal fluid. *Journal of Neurology, Neurosurgery and Psychiatry,* **44,** 323–328.

REPLY

TONES AND STATES

Elliott M. Blass and Vivian Ciaramitaro

As is his wont, Ronald G. Barr has raised a number of important, thought-provoking issues about this *Monograph* that demand further explication. Much of his Commentary focused on the issue of *state* and, implicitly, on our failure to come to grips with this issue. His points are well taken. As Barr points out, we distinguished between taste and pacifier effects on state, the former causing a fundamental change, the latter only a change, hardly a rigorous distinction.

There are at least two problems in the way that we have dealt with state changes, and Barr addresses them both. One is a problem in measurement: Do the descriptions of "on-off" and "graded" capture process or do they reflect characteristics of the measure or the experimental paradigm? This is a concern that we share. The second concern is the use of the term "state." Although Barr raises a number of problems with the term, he does not offer a solution. His articulate presentation of the problems has encouraged us to attempt a resolution. We suggest dropping the term "state" as an explanatory or unifying concept and present other means of accounting for the data that are more precise and testable.

Let us address the first issue. The strategy of our research has been to be alert for differences between the effects of taste (flavor) and of tactile stimulation and, on finding and replicating them between species and among different measures, to evaluate the predictions that different underlying mechanisms make. Thus, our original hypothesis was that the time course of gustatory stimulation differed from that of orotactile stimulation in its control of behavioral change. This formulation allowed us to dissociate opioid from nonopioid mediation; the systems were seen as dichotomous. Although a single, continuous measure, time in this case, is a difficult metric with which to distinguish graded from on-off systems, there has not been any overlap in recovery times among different measures for recovery from sucrose as opposed to pacifier stimulation.

Employing multiple converging studies helps soften Barr's criticism. It does not eliminate it, however, because the only dependent measure for a graded effect in these paradigms is time (neurophysiologists, in contrast, can use firing rate; psychobiologists can see graded differences in running speed, etc.). It is possible that our indices, which are all time based, share this common flaw. The best that can be done under the circumstances is to make specific predictions about the operating characteristics of taste (opioid) and tactile (nonopioid) systems under different experimental conditions.

One such evaluation, for example, concerns the decay of sucrose effectiveness over time. In studying reduction in crying induced by sucrose during blood collection for PKU (phenylketonuria) evaluation, Blass and Shah (1994) have discovered that 2 min was the most effective delay between termination of sucrose intake and the initiation of blood collection, more effective than 30, 60, or 90 sec, arguing against protracted effectiveness resulting from lingering sucrose taste and arguing for a characteristic of the system. Thus, given the number of replications between species and among paradigms, what started as a tentative hypothesis has taken on the status of a system characteristic. Findings that do not accord at first blush might be better understood through different explanatory systems. In a way, Barr has acknowledged this in his attentional explanation for the disruption of crying by quinine.

The second issue, state, is more substantive. Here we were guilty of "lumping" disparate findings into one explanatory construct. At an early point in the analysis of behavior and its underlying mechanisms, lumping presents a trap of utilizing a single function to explain findings that may be better understood through multiple functions. Barr rightly pointed out the awkwardness of our distinction between "state changes" and "fundamental state changes." We fell into the trap. A more defensible approach to the problem of newborn behavior and physiology is presented in Figure R1 and justified below.

First, state is used to describe behavior. It has neither an explanatory nor a unifying function. We prefer the notion of central excitation to indicate a neural system that is arousing and energy expending. When it crosses threshold, it results in all the characteristics that we have described in normal infants during crying and that are diagnostic in cocaine and methadone infants: crying, hyperactivity, and tachycardia. The opioids affect this system in two ways. First, on the basis of the crying, hyperactivity, and tachycardia profiles of methadone and cocaine infants, there is an opioid input that, when available, tonically dampens the excitatory system. Second, on the basis of the responsiveness of normal rat and human infants to sucrose,

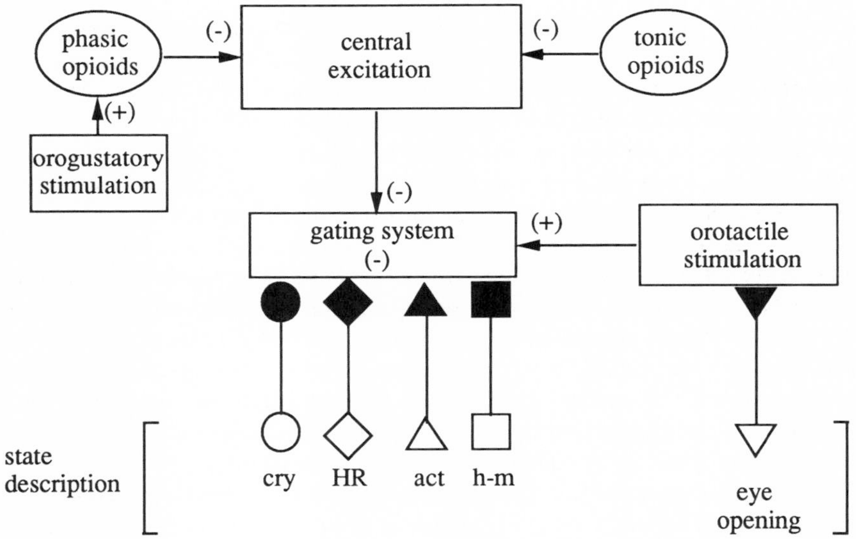

FIG. R1.—A model that specifies the effects of various manipulations on the behavior of infant rats and newborn humans. At the core of the model is a central excitatory state that, when above threshold, elicits crying, enhances gross motor activity, and causes tachycardia by inhibiting the gating system. It interferes with hand-mouth coordination. Opioids tonically inhibit this system in normal infants. It can also be inhibited phasically through orogustatory stimulation. Orotactile stimulation excites the gating system through nonopioid pathways. Each effector system is presented individually. The filled symbols represent the operating characteristics of each effector and the open symbols the observable manifestation of the synergism among excitation, gating, and effector systems. This manifestation is referred to as "state." "State" is a descriptive term in the model. It does *not* have any explanatory function because it does not identify any of the parameters of the model or specify where or how a physiological or an environmental influence is acting.

other sugars, and milk and the *in*ability of cocaine or methadone infants or naltrexone-treated rats to do the same, there is also a phasic opioid stimulation that further dampens the energy-expending system. The central excitatory system inhibits the gating system according to the model. The gating system itself is inhibitory. Thus, by inhibiting the inhibitor, the central excitatory system exaggerates crying, activity, and heart rate.

Third, on the basis of the normal responses of methadone and cocaine infants and naltrexone-injected rats to orotactile stimulation, we suggest that the nonopioid forms of stimulation in both normal and opioid-deficient humans and animals excite the gating system (i.e., increase inhibition). Such stimulation does not directly affect the high-energy system because of the rapid reinstatement of crying, activity, and tachycardia. According to Smith, Fillion, and Blass (1990), the pre- and poststimulation levels of crying are significantly correlated. This also speaks to a separate target for orotactile stimulation. The lack of "savings" in this system can be further appreciated in the methadone infant, whose heart rate peaked at 215 BPM (beats per minute) within 30 sec of pacifier removal. We have seen comparable reactions in cocaine infants (Blass, Ciaramitaro, & Jain, 1994).

Fourth, the outputs of individual effectors are presented separately. The filled symbols represent each effector's operating characteristics. The open symbols represent the interactions among the central-excitatory system, the gating mechanism, and the intrinsic characteristics of the effector in question. It is the open symbols that provide the observable data. Without pursuing it in detail, note that the operating characteristics of the h-m (hand-mouth) system must differ from those of crying, heart rate, and activity because hand-mouth behavior is reduced when they are increased and increased when the others are reduced. Note too that eye opening is not a property of the gating system but is uniquely linked to orotactile stimulation because sucrose does not elicit eye opening in newborns.

This conceptualization holds a number of advantages over descriptions that use state terms. First, it provides at least three mechanisms through which central tone with its accompanying high-energy output can be modulated. This means that experimental hypotheses can be tested with considerably more rigor than with a single term of state. The findings that Barr reports from his own lab are amenable to this form of analysis. The quinine data focus on *attention* as a possible mediator in arresting crying. Through which mechanism? Would it stop crying if administered on a pacifier? Would the infant start to cry again if she became calm through pacifier sucking? How would quinine work in cocaine or methadone infants? Why is it a source of displeasure in already calm infants? Answering these questions may help us better understand the development of orogustatory motivation. Is it possible that increased activity in the energy-expending system affects gustatory perception? If so, does this change developmentally so that quinine is rejected by older infants regardless of the characteristic of the energy-expending system? This may be possible when one considers that infant rats work to receive shock that just a few days later they will find aversive (Camp & Rudy, 1987). The frame of reference that Figure R1 provides allows for precise questions to be asked concerning this phenomenon within a framework that starts to evaluate the mechanisms that underlie newborn and infant affective development.

A second advantage of the present approach is that, by starting with three variables and stating each of their properties, the model is open to evaluating behavioral patterns that fall *outside* the domains that it provides. This allows us to enrich our understanding of the central mediation of affect in a systematic, data-driven fashion.

Thus comes our reluctance to continue using the term "state." We can use the notion of a high-energy output system for newborns that embraces all the findings of the current studies and the cocaine studies as well. As soon as it is demonstrated that the high-energy system does not have to have a crying component to it, either developmentally in older infants or in different cases for newborns, then the model can be modified. At present, however, it is consistent with the behavioral, pharmacological, and temporal findings and provides a framework for testing additional hypotheses.

References

Blass, E. M., Ciaramitaro, V., & Jain, A. (1994). *Cocaine and calming in human newborns: Differential effects of a pacifier and of sucrose on crying, heart rate, activity, and eye opening.* Manuscript submitted for publication.

Blass, E. M., & Shah, A. (1994). *Pain reducing properties of sucrose in human newborns.* Manuscript submitted for publication.

Camp, L. L., & Rudy, J. W. (1987). Changes in the categorization of appetitive and aversive events during postnatal development of the rat. *Developmental Psychobiology,* **21,** 25–42.

Smith, B. A., Fillion, T. J., & Blass, E. M. (1990). Orally-mediated sources of calming in one to three day-old human infants. *Developmental Psychology,* **26**(5), 731–737.

CONTRIBUTORS

Elliott M. Blass (Ph.D. 1969, University of Virginia) is professor of psychology and nutrition at Cornell University. He has previously taught at the Johns Hopkins University. His research focuses on the structure of motivation in neonatal humans and rats, on the short- and long-term biological and behavioral consequences of mother-infant interactions, and on the mechanisms underlying those interactions.

Vivian Ciaramitaro (M.S. 1993, University of Pennsylvania) is currently pursuing her Ph.D. at the Institute of Neurological Sciences of the University of Pennsylvania. Her research interests include cognitive development and animal models for the anatomical, behavioral, and molecular substrates of movement disorders and recovery of function.

Ronald G. Barr (M.D.C.M. 1975, McGill University) is professor of pediatrics and psychiatry at the McGill University Faculty of Medicine and head of the Child Development Programme at Montreal Children's Hospital. His research interests focus on dysfunctional syndromes in children, with particular interest in cross-disciplinary approaches to understanding "biobehavioral" determinants of crying, colic, and pain behaviors and of attentional disorders.

STATEMENT OF EDITORIAL POLICY

The *Monographs* series is intended as an outlet for major reports of developmental research that generate authoritative new findings and use these to foster a fresh and/or better-integrated perspective on some conceptually significant issue or controversy. Submissions from programmatic research projects are particularly welcome; these may consist of individually or group-authored reports of findings from some single large-scale investigation or of a sequence of experiments centering on some particular question. Multiauthored sets of independent studies that center on the same underlying question can also be appropriate; a critical requirement in such instances is that the various authors address common issues and that the contribution arising from the set as a whole be both unique and substantial. In essence, irrespective of how it may be framed, any work that contributes significant data and/or extends developmental thinking will be taken under editorial consideration.

Submissions should contain a minimum of 80 manuscript pages (including tables and references); the upper limit of 150–175 pages is much more flexible (please submit four copies; a copy of every submission and associated correspondence is deposited eventually in the archives of the SRCD). Neither membership in the Society for Research in Child Development nor affiliation with the academic discipline of psychology are relevant; the significance of the work in extending developmental theory and in contributing new empirical information is by far the most crucial consideration. Because the aim of the series is not only to advance knowledge on specialized topics but also to enhance cross-fertilization among disciplines or subfields, it is important that the links between the specific issues under study and larger questions relating to developmental processes emerge as clearly to the general reader as to specialists on the given topic.

Potential authors who may be unsure whether the manuscript they are planning would make an appropriate submission are invited to draft an outline of what they propose and send it to the Editor for assessment. This mechanism, as well as a more detailed description of all editorial policies, evaluation processes, and format requirements, is given in the "Guidelines for the Preparation of *Monographs* Submissions," which can be obtained by writing to the Editor designate, Rachel K. Clifton, Department of Psychology, University of Massachusetts, Amherst, MA 01003.